Journey To The Center Of The Earth

ISBN : 2-8302-1606-7

© EBSA

© 1985, American version, Edito-Service S.A., Geneva

In collaboration with Margrace Corporation, New Jersey
Omniprose Ltd. Toronto

03 092 003 (03)

CHAPTER 1

One Sunday morning, toward the end of May, Martha, my uncle's cook, had the shock of her life: her master had just returned home one hour earlier than usual. The poor woman, who had barely begun her preparations for the meal, cried:

"What? Are you back already?"

It seemed to me that my uncle must have some very good reason for this unheard-of change in his rigid routine.

"Mr. Axel," said Martha, "I'll leave it to you to make your uncle see reason!"

And, turning on her heel, she hurried back to her kitchen.

I was much too timid to question Professor Otto Lidenbrock's actions, let alone stand up to him, for I knew better than anyone how irritable and unpredictable he could be.

I heard the front door slam behind him. His heavy footsteps shook the wooden stairs, then he marched through the dining room and rushed into his study.

"Axel! Come up here!"

He spoke sharply and I hurried to obey.

My uncle's study was more like a museum, containing innumerable samples of minerals, all meticulously labeled and cataloged. Every one was familiar to me as, in my childhood, instead of playing with boys of my own age, I had passed many absorbing hours sorting specimens of graphite, anthracite, coal, lignite and peat into jars and bottles, some white, others made of colored glass. I would spend hours studying a piece of metal, whether iron or gold, seeing it only as another scientific specimen.

But, as I walked into the room that day, I gave no thought to all these wonders. My uncle was ensconced

1. The impossible alphabet of the god Odin!

Professor Otto Lindenbrock is my uncle, and I was in his dining room one Sunday morning when . . .

Master Axel! Master Axel!

What is it, Martha? Why are you so upset?

I've only just begun preparing lunch and your uncle is already home!

Ah well! If he's hungry he'll soon let us know. He's always in such a hurry!

My uncle was such an impatient man that he even tried to make his house-plants grow faster by tugging at their leaves each morning!

I don't know, they don't seem to be growing at all!

Although he was abrupt, irritable and miserly, he was not a bad man and he had a world-famous reputation as a mineralogist.

PROFESSOR OTTO LIDENBROCK TREATISE ON TRANSCENDENTAL CRYSTALLOGRAPHY

Martha hurried back to her kitchen. I was about to creep back to my room, when . . .

Axel!

Before I had a chance to move the professor called again . . .

Come on! You should be here by now!

I ran to his study . . .

What a book, Axel! What a book!

Another of the old bookworm's finds! He's only interested in books that are incomprehensible and unreadable!

Axel, this is Snorre Turleson's "Heims-Kringla". It dates from the twelfth century and is an account of the Norwegian princes who reigned in Iceland.

Marvelous!

It's a very handsome volume...

What's that got to do with it, my boy? It was written by hand using the Runic alphabet, it's unique!

The Runic alphabet is believed to have been invented by the god Odin, and it was used by the ancient Scandinavians. See how beautiful it is, Axel!

in a deep armchair, holding a book on his lap.

"What a book! What a book!" he muttered.

His seemingly exaggerated delight reminded me that, besides teaching mineralogy at Hamburg University, Professor Lidenbrock was also a booklover in his spare time. To put it more accurately, a book had no value in his eyes unless it were unique, or at the very least considered unreadable by the average person.

"Can't you see, Axel," he said, "that this is a priceless treasure, a wonderfully rare work? I came across it this very morning in Hevelius' bookshop!"

"Splendid!" I replied, trying to appear overcome with awe.

"Is that all you can say?"

With a hint of reproach in his voice, he continued:

"This wonderful volume is the *Heims-Kringla* of Snorre Turleson, the famous twelfth-century Icelandic author! It's the chronicle of the Norwegian princes who ruled over Iceland."

"I presume it's a translation, Uncle," I hazarded, pretending to be interested.

"A translation!" roared the Professor. "You obviously have no notion of the importance of this book. It is the original edition in Icelandic. Hand-written! Runic!"

I must have looked utterly baffled, for my uncle rose to his feet, came over to me, and said in a scornful tone:

"And now I suppose you're going to ask me what that means?"

I answered pompously, as though my pride were injured:

"Of course not!"

Taking no notice, the Professor began to give me a lecture on a subject which left me completely cold.

"Then I shall tell you," he declared with aplomb. "The Runic alphabet was used long ago in Iceland and Scandinavia. Legend has it that Odin, the god of poetry, wisdom and war, was its inventor."

I was very interested in tales of gods and princes, and was about to say so to my uncle, when a scrap of parchment slipped out of the book. My uncle pounced upon it, and carefully unfolded it on the table. It measured about five inches by three, and it bore a few lines of strange, stick-like signs.

The Professor adjusted his spectacles, stared at the parchment for some minutes, then declared with a satisfied smile:

"Yes, they are runes! They're absolutely identical to the ones in Snorre Turleson's manuscript. But . . .

2. A tall man with a long thin nose and two bulging eyes...

what on earth do they mean?"

He started to quiver with emotion.

"It's ancient Icelandic, I'm sure of it!"

He should have known, if anyone did, for he was something of a linguist. He spoke, or at least had a working knowledge of, a fair number of the two thousand languages and four thousand dialects used on the five continents. Faced with this puzzle, he was obviously going to lose his temper, and I was waiting for an outburst of violent anger when the clock struck two, and our cook opened the door to announce:

"The soup is ready!"

"The devil take you, your soup, and anyone who eats it!" my uncle cried.

Martha beat a hasty retreat, and I hurried after her to take my place in the dining room. The Professor did not join us. To my knowledge, it was the first time that he had missed a meal. And what a meal! Parsley soup, a ham omelette with sorrel garnish, veal with plum sauce, a fruit tart, and a fine Moselle wine to wash it all down with. My uncle was prepared to forego such a feast for the sake of a musty old piece of parchment! Being a dutiful and affectionate nephew, I precluded any unpleasantness between my uncle and the cook by eating his share too.

"I've never known such a thing!" complained Martha. "He loves his food so much, and yet here he is, turning his nose up at it!"

"It really is most peculiar!" I agreed.

"Mr. Axel, I must speak plain. No good will come of this!"

I was eating my dessert when a terrible roar tore me away from the fruit tart. I jumped up and ran to my uncle's study.

"Come in!" he said, without further ado. "I am now positive that we are dealing with a runic text. But it hides some secret, and I am determined to decipher it, come what may."

Striking the table with his fist, he barked:

"Sit down!"

I obeyed.

"Find a pen! I'm going to dictate the text, substituting the corresponding letters from our alphabet for the ancient Icelandic ones written here. We'll see then if it makes sense. But be careful not to make any mistakes!"

The dictation began:

m.rnlls	esreuel	seecJde
sgtssmf	unteief	niedrke
kt,samn	atrateS	Saodrrn
emtnaeI	nuaect	rrilSa
Atvaar	.nscrc	ieaabs

| ccdrmi | eeutul | frantum |
| dt,iac | oseibo | KediiY |

When I had finished, the Professor snatched up the paper on which I had written, examined it closely, then said with a puzzled air:

"What can it possibly mean?"

As I had learned never to interrupt him, I kept silent.

My uncle was lost in thought, and would have had little interest in my opinion, even if I had had one to offer, which I did not. He spoke at last:

"It's what the experts call a cryptogram. The letters have been jumbled up according to some system or other, and if we can put them back in the original order, we will find they have some meaning. To think I might be holding the clue to some great discovery! All that remains is to find the key."

Picking up the parchment and the book, he compared them.

"They aren't in the same handwriting. The cryptogram is of a later date than the book. Look, the first letter is a double 'm', which doesn't figure in Turleson's text, because it wasn't added to the Icelandic alphabet until the fourteenth century. That means that at least two centuries separate these two texts. What do you think, Axel?"

I replied that his reasoning seemed sound.

"I imagine," continued the Professor, "that one of the previous owners of the book wrote this mysterious text. I wonder if he wrote his name somewhere in the book?"

Removing his eyeglasses, my uncle examined the book carefully through a powerful magnifying glass. On the back of the second page he noticed what looked like an ink blot but, on closer examination, proved to be a line of faint writing. He traced the letters through a thin piece of paper and suddenly cried out:

"Arne Saknussemm! He was a famous sixteenth–century Icelandic alchemist!"

I couldn't help looking at my uncle with a certain admiration.

This mention of gods and princes excited my interest, and I was about to say as much to my uncle, when . . .

What on earth is this?

Little did I know that this scrap of parchment was to persuade my uncle and myself to set off on one of the most fantastic expeditions of all time.

These are Runes, similar to the ones in Turleson's book. But what do they mean?

At that moment . . .

The soup is ready!

The devil take the soup and the woman who cooked it!

Martha left the room and I followed her to the dining room where I ate my lunch with relish!

It's the first time I've known your uncle to miss a meal! No good will come of it!

I hope he doesn't fly into a temper when he sees that I've eaten his share.

Axel! . . .

Oh no, not again!

My uncle dictated to me the modern letters corresponding to the Runes on the parchment . . .

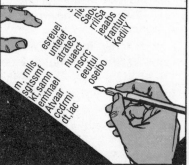

It must be in code. The letters have been jumbled up to make it unintelligible. At least two hundred years separate the book from the parchment. Who did the book belong to? The owner must be the man who wrote down this message.

The professor examined the book with his magnifying glass and . . .

Look! I've found a name on the back of the second page, Arne Saknussemm! He was a famous 16th-century Icelandic alchemist!

CHAPTER 2

Axel, the Professor Lindenbrock's nephew, is a smart but very shy young man.

Picture a tall, thin man in excellent health, nearing fifty, but looking ten years younger, with bulging eyes that kept darting to and fro, and a long thin nose. He walked with long strides, his fists clenched, a sure sign of his impetuous and sometimes irritable nature.

Otto Lidenbrock, a lecturer in mineralogy at Hamburg University, was also the curator of the mineralogical museum founded by the former Russian ambassador to the Prussian court. He was not a bad man, but definitely weird. You could be sure that he would lose his temper at least once or twice during every lecture. To tell the truth, he didn't care whether his students worked hard or whether they passed their exams. He was convinced that he was always right, and could not stand contradiction. Although he had a treasure–house of knowledge, he tried to keep it to himself as much as possible.

Unfortunately for him, the Professor had difficulty in speaking fluently. In the middle of a lecture he would be brought up short by a word, and would be unable to continue. He would wrestle with it, stammer, and finally roar with anger when his students began to giggle. In his defence it must be said that many mineralogical terms, half Greek and half Latin, are very difficult to pronounce: they would take the skin off even a poet's lips!

Despite being mocked for this slight infirmity and feared for his temper, my uncle was universally respected as one of the world's greatest mineralogists. With his hammer, steel pointer, magnetic needle, blowpipe and bottle of nitric acid, he had no equal in classifying any given mineral from the six hundred types known to modern science. To do this, he would analyze the appearance, hardness, sound, smell and even the taste of a mineral. His instinct and knowledge in this field were unrivaled. Many learned men would make a point of calling on him to ask his opinion if ever they passed through Hamburg. Because of this, the name of Lidenbrock was known and respected in scientific circles throughout the world. He was also responsible for several remarkable discoveries. In 1853, his *Treatise on Transcendental Crystallography* appeared in Leipzig. This imposing volume, with its colored plates, cost the publisher dear, as he failed to cover his costs.

As a University Professor, my uncle was quite well off. The brick and wood house on Königsstrasse belonged to him. True, it was not exactly perpendicular, with slightly bulging walls, and wearing its roof a little askew, like a student's cap, but thanks to an old elm, whose spreading branches supported the front wall, the house stood firm.

My uncle shared his home with his ward Graüben, a charming seventeen-year-old with blue eyes; Martha, his faithful servant; and myself, his orphaned nephew. I worked as his laboratory assistant, while he helped me with my studies. Knowing that I had the blood of a mineralogist in my veins, I never felt bored in the company of the pebbles and rocks which lined the shelves.

Life was happy enough in that little house, despite the master's fits of temper. My uncle, although he would never admit it, was fond of me in his way. His main fault was that he was incapable of waiting, which sometimes led to comical situations. For example, when he planted seedlings in pots in his study, he kept tugging at the leaves to make them grow faster! This rough sketch of my uncle will make it easier for the reader to understand the Professor's subsequent actions.

To return to the parchment and the manuscript, the Professor's lively imagination was leading him to form all sorts of theories.

"The alchemists were the only real scientists at that time. This Saknussemm was a very clever man, and it may be that he concealed some important discovery in this cryptogram."

"Sure, but why would he have kept it to himself?"

"I don't know why, but I'm determined to find out. I shall not rest until I have decoded the message."

"That seems a bit extreme," I said, rather daringly.

My uncle withered me with a look and said threateningly:

"And neither will you, because I shall need you to help me!"

And, giving me no time to reply, he rushed on:

● The Professor has difficulty in speaking fluently.

●● His ward Graüben, his nephew Axel and Martha, his servant.

●●● She was to come back within a few days.

"The first thing we must do is to identify the language he used for the message. That shouldn't prove too difficult."

I opened my mouth to object, but my uncle went on talking to himself:

"When Saknussemm was not writing in his mother tongue, he would probably have used Latin. All the educated men of the sixteenth century were fluent in that language, so this is what we shall try first."

I sat up with a jolt. I wasn't long out of school and could see no similarity between the barbarous message I had written down and the lyrical language of Virgil and Horace.

The Professor picked up the dictated passage and looked at it again.

"We have here a series of one hundred and thirty-two letters in apparent disorder. Some seem to be grouped in consonants, others in vowels. This arrangement is obviously intentional. The original sentence was written out sensibly, and was then scrambled, using some code which I have yet to discover . . . . But what is the key to it, Axel?"

I did not reply, and with good reason. My eyes were glued to a portrait on the wall of Graüben, my uncle's young ward. At that time she was staying with relatives, but she was due to return to Hamburg within a few days. I was very much in love with her, and was waiting impatiently to see her again. We shared the same interests, the same passion for mineralogy, and we had decided to marry as soon as we finished our studies. The smiling face of my charming fiancée instantly transported me far from the realities of everyday life, but my uncle, thumping the table with his fist, brought me quickly back to earth:

"If you wanted to mix up the letters in a secret message," he said, pursuing his line of thought, "the first thing you would do would be to write the words vertically. This is what you must do. Take a sheet of paper, and write any sentence you like, but put the letters in vertical columns, grouping them in fives or sixes."

Without further thought, I wrote:

I	o	m	y	e	e
l	u	u	I	G	n
o	v	c	i	r	!
v	e	h	t	a	
e	r	,	t	ü	
y	y	m	I	b	

"Good!" said the Professor, without even a glance at my work. "Now set the groups of letters out in a

3. He slammed the door and made everything rock!

But if the parchment contains some secret, why did Saknussemm go to such trouble to hide it!

Didn't Galileo do the same? I shan't rest until I find the key to this document. I shall neither eat nor sleep until I have discovered it!

I'm glad I ate double rations at lunch time!

I wonder which language he used for the message? From the ratio of vowels to consonants I'd be willing to bet that it's a romance language. Latin most probably!

Some of these groups of letters consist entirely of consonants, while others have only vowels. Therefore one group of letters cannot be juggled about to make a word. The original sentence was probably written out normally and was then jumbled up using some system or other. There must be a solution. But what the devil is it?

13

I was not listening. My eyes were glued to the portrait of Graüben, my uncle's ward. We had become engaged without his knowledge, keenly aware that my uncle was utterly incapable of understanding an emotion like love.

A loud rap on the table brought me back to earth.

Axel, instead of standing there dreaming, find a piece of paper and a pen and write any sentence you like in vertical columns.

I obeyed automatically and wrote . . .

Then my uncle asked me to write each horizontal line as a word . . .

Now that looks very like the arrangement of letters on the parchment: vowels and consonants are all mixed up. To read the sentence one must take the first letter of each word, then the second, the third and so on. I shall now read your original sentence . . .

"I love you very much, my little Graüben!" What? You love her?

Yes er no . . .

Fortunately, he immediately returned to studying the document, and dictated the letters on the parchment one by one, using the same system that we had tried with my embarrassing sentence.

mmessunkaSenrA. icefdoK. segnittamurtn ecertserrette, rotaivsa dua, ednecsedsadne lacart niiiluJsiratracSarbmutab iledmek meretar csiluco Y sleffenSnI

horizontal line."

I obeyed, and obtained the following result:

Iomyee luullGn ovcir! vehta er,tü yymlb

"Splendid!" cried my uncle. "Now, to read the sentence which you have just written, all I need to do is to take the first letter of each word, then the second, and so on."

To his great surprise, and even more to mine, he read out:

" 'I love you very much, my little Graüben!' What's this? You're in love with Graüben?"

"Er . . . yes . . . that is . . . no . . ."

"Good! Well, now, let's apply my method to our document!" he declared.

The importance of his current problem had already banished my unfortunate choice of sentence from his thoughts.

Putting on his spectacles again, he set to work on a problem which was of little importance or interest to me. He gave a loud cough, then, in a solemn voice, dictated a new version, taking the first letter of each word, then the second:

mmessunkaSenrA.icefdoK.segnittamurtn
ecertserrette, rotaivsadua, ednecsedsadne
lacartniiiluJsiratracSarbmutabiledmek
meretarcsilucoYsleffenSnI

By the time he had finished I was eager to learn the result of the experiment, but, instead of the Latin which I was expecting, I heard the Professor exclaim furiously:

"That can't be it! It makes no sense at all!"

A blow from my uncle's fist on the table made the inkstand rock: ink spurted into the air, and the pen flew out of my hand. Then, hurtling across the room like a cannonball, my uncle rushed out of the door, took the stairs four at a time, and stormed out into the street.

When the front door was slammed shut, shaking the whole house from top to bottom, Martha ran up to me in a panic:

"Has he gone?" she asked.

"Yes," I replied. "And don't expect him for supper. My uncle has decided to go without food until he finds the solution to his current problem!"

"You don't mean it, Mr. Axel!"

"I'm afraid I do, Martha. The Professor is going to starve us, for as long as it takes him to decipher some old scrawl!"

"We'll die of hunger!" the poor woman exclaimed, lifting her arms up to heaven as she returned to the kitchen.

● The message was expected in Latin.
●● A man had been bold and mad enough . . . to make a journey to the center of the earth!

Back in my uncle's study I picked up the sheet of paper, but no matter how often I read the columns of letters, I could find no sense or clue in them. However, I did manage to decipher the English word "ice" in the first line, and below that the Latin words "rota", "mutabile", "ira", "nec" and "atra". These last seemed to confirm my uncle's theory that the text was originally written in Latin.

In the fourth line, I found another word: "luco", which means a sacred wood; in the third, the Hebrew word "tabiled", and in the last line the words "mer", "arc" and "mère", which are pure French.

It was enough to drive a man mad. Four different languages in one and the same sentence; it defied belief! What connection could there possibly be between such a jumble of words as these?

The more different combinations I tried, the further I seemed to be from a solution. The letters started to dance before my eyes and the effort of juggling them around seemed to induce a hallucination.

I felt stifled, and used the sheet of paper as a fan. Suddenly, as I saw first the back, then the front of the sheet in quick succession, Latin words seemed to appear, among them "craterem" and "terrestre".

4. Is this message a joke?

Light dawned: I had found the key! To understand the meaning of the text, it was not even necessary to read it through the back of the paper. The Professor's theories seemed to be correct. He was right about the arrangement of the letters, right about the language used. He had needed only a little something extra to read the Latin sentence straight through from beginning to end, and it was just this "something" that luck had helped me to find.

I made myself walk slowly round the room twice, in an attempt to calm myself down, then I leaned over the paper once more, placing my finger on each letter in succession, and read the whole sentence aloud.

It was a frightening revelation! I was flabbergasted by the discovery I had just made. A man had . . . had been bold and mad enough to . . . to make a journey to the center of the earth!

Almost beside myself with apprehension and excitement, I cried:

"I'm going to keep this to myself! My uncle must never find out! If he discovers that such a journey has been made, he is sure to want to follow suit. He might easily find the key to the puzzle, so I had better destroy the documents."

I was about to throw them on the fire but, just as I walked over to the hearth, the study door opened, and in walked my uncle. Fortunately, I was able to replace the parchment and our workings on the table without being seen. The Professor seemed depressed and preoccupied. Without a word to me, he sat down in his armchair, picked up a sheet of paper and began to write down figures and formulae.

This continued for three long hours. Engrossed in his work, he would rub out, begin again, cross out, start again, oblivious of everything around him. He was so absorbed that he did not even notice that it had grown dark. He therefore looked up in surprise when Martha daringly opened the door, put her head round it, and asked nervously:

"Are you having your supper tonight, sir?"

As no reply was forthcoming, she shut the door and crept away.

As for me, after a long fight to stay awake, I found myself falling asleep on the couch, while my uncle Lidenbrock went on with his calculations.

It's nonsense! Roared my uncle and, slamming the door, he left the house.

BLAM!

Martha ran up to me in a panic . . .

My uncle has decreed that we shall starve until he has deciphered a secret message!

Heaven help us! We'll die of hunger!

Faced with this miserable prospect, I worked feverishly on the text. I felt stifled and used the sheet of paper as a fan. Suddenly . . .

Oh! Seeing the front and the back of the parchment in quick succession I thought I saw some Latin words. There was "craterem" and "terrestre"!

I had found the key to the puzzle! I didn't even have to go to the trouble of reading the message through the back of the paper. My uncle's theory was correct. The language was, as he thought, Latin, and he had hit on the right system for unscrambling the letters. It had only needed a little something extra for him to decipher the sentence and by chance I had stumbled on just that "something".

I had discovered the secret of the parchment simply by looking at it!

Is it possible that this man really did what he describes here? My uncle must never know . . .

Well, I can put a stop to that. Even if I say nothing, my uncle will solve the problem sooner or later. I think I had better burn the parchment!

If he finds out, he's sure to want to set off at once. That's the sort of man he is. The worst is that he'd take me with him and I don't want to go.

I was about to do so

When my uncle came in. I just managed to put the documents back in time. . . .

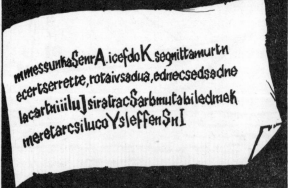

mmessunkaSenrA.icefdoK.segnittamurtn
ecertserrette,rotaivsadua,ednecsedsadne
lacartniiilu]siratracSarbmutabiledmek
meretarcsilucoYsleffenSnI

CHAPTER 3

When I opened my eyes next morning, the Professor was still hard at work. His red eyes, drawn features, tousled hair, and the fact that, contrary to his usual practice, he had not shaved, showed how determined he was to break the code. All it needed was one word from me and his torment would be over, but I said nothing.

"I'll keep it to myself!" I repeated over and over again. "If he thought he could do something no other geologist had done, my uncle would throw caution to the winds and, if the case arose, would gladly risk his life. I will not be responsible for his death!"

Otto Lidenbrock worked on, giving his imagination free rein. Oblivious to his surroundings, he was living in a world where he felt at home, and which seemed to give him the satisfaction he sought. Towards noon, I began to feel sharp hunger pangs. Martha had used up the last of the food in the larder the day before and wanted to go shopping, but she could not get out of the house: the doorkey was in the Professor's pocket and the good woman did not dare disturb him.

I realized that I could not let this uncomfortable situation drag on much longer. It reminded me of a time, some years previously, when my uncle had been working on his great mineralogical encyclopedia: that time he went forty-eight hours without food! Under protest, Martha and I had had to do likewise. I began to wonder whether I was not attaching too much importance to the document, and thought that perhaps my uncle would not agree with my conclusions and that he might dismiss the message as a joke . . . The more I mulled it over, the more it seemed to me that the Professor would, in any case, eventually find the solution, and if he came to it by his own efforts,

● When he was working on his great mineralogical encyclopedia.

Martha, Graüben and I would have the almost hopeless task of dissuading him from dashing off on a journey which was sheer madness from the start.

In short, all the arguments I had rejected the night before now seemed reasonable and I resolved to come clean.

5. He clutched his head in his hands, snatched a pencil...

I was wondering how to raise the subject when the Professor abruptly rose to his feet, pushed back his chair and walked over to the door.

Terrified that he might leave the house and lock the door again behind him, I called:

"Uncle!"

He seemed not to hear me.

"Uncle!" I repeated, raising my voice and going over to him.

"Eh?" he said, as though roused from a deep sleep.

"Do you have the key?"

"Which key? The one to the front door?"

"No, Uncle, the key to the cryptogram!"

He peered at me over his eyeglasses and obviously saw something odd in my expression, for he gripped my arm and looked at me with a question in his eyes.

I nodded.

My uncle shook his head with a sort of condescending pity, as if he were dealing with a madman.

I nodded again, but more vigorously this time.

The Professor's eyes glistened menacingly and I could tell that he was keeping a tight rein on his emotions.

This mute conversation lasted for some minutes. I did not know what to do; I dared not speak or move, for fear that the Professor might smother me in his transports of joy. Suddenly, he broke the silence by saying:

"Well . . . this key . . .?"

"Yes . . . by chance . . . look, Uncle," I stammered, showing him the sheet of paper on which I had written out his dictation.

"It's meaningless!" he answered, crumpling the paper into a ball.

"It is, if you read it from the beginning. But if you read it backwards . . ."

He hardly let me finish the sentence before he gave a cry, or rather a roar. The light had dawned and he was transfigured.

"So," declared the Professor, "Saknussemm had the bright idea of writing his message backward! Imagine! The thought never occurred to me!"

He smoothed the sheet of paper and, his voice shaking with emotion, read the whole document back-

● The message has been written backwards.

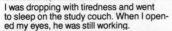

ward. When he had finished, he asked me to write out the translation:

Descend into the crater of Sneffels Yokul, over which the shadow of Scartaris falls before the calends of July, bold traveler, and you will reach the center of the earth. I did this.
Arne Saknussemm.

My uncle was beside himself with joy. "He paced up and down, clutched his head in his hands, stood up, sat down, snatched a pencil, scribbled a few lines, moved the chairs around, piled up his books. He was so excited he did not know what to do. At last he calmed down and, overcome with exhaustion after his night–long vigil and ceaseless toil, he collapsed into his armchair.

"What time is it?" he asked, after a few moments' silence.

"Three o'clock," I replied.

"What's that? Three o'clock?"

"Yes, Uncle."

"But I'm starved! We should have eaten ages ago! Afterwards . . . . "

"Yes, Uncle?"

"Afterwards, Martha can pack my trunk . . . yours, too, while she's about it.

"Why?"

"We're leaving!" replied the Professor, in a determined tone, and made his way to the dining room.

I could see at once that only well–reasoned arguments and scientific considerations could sway him from seeing this journey through. Even if there was a way to the center of the earth, as this Icelandic alchemist seemed to believe, it was sheer folly to attempt such a journey. However, for the moment, it seemed easier and wiser to make no comment or objection.

Lunch lasted longer than usual. During the meal, my uncle was almost jovial. He even went so far as to make a few harmless jokes, something I had never known him do before. After the dessert, he beckoned me to follow him to his study.

I obeyed. He sat down at the table, cleared a space, and invited me to sit down facing him.

"Axel," he said gently, "you are a bright boy and I shall not forget the help you have given me in this business. Your intelligence has saved me precious time. I shall remember it and you will share in the glory we are to win."

He paused for a moment, then went on:

"Above all, I would ask you not to breathe a word of our secret. You must be well aware that the world of science harbors some envious men. Many of my colleagues would jump at the chance of making this journey! But they must learn nothing until we return."

"If we return!" I muttered.

My uncle did not hear this, or at least pretended not to have heard. He took down an atlas from the shelves, opened it and declared:

"Here is one of the best maps of Iceland. I think it will give us the information we require."

I bent over the map.

"Can you see," asked my uncle, "this island dotted with volcanoes? You will notice that they all bear the same legend: 'Yokul', which means 'lacier' in Iceland-ic. In fact, although nearly all of them are still active, the majority are blanketed in a thick layer of ice, hence the description."

"But what does Sneffels mean?"

"Sneffels is a mountain some five thousand feet high, one of the most remarkable in Iceland. If what the parchment says is true, and it does lead to the center of the earth, then its fame will be world-wide!"

"I don't see how it can be true!" I cried.

"Not true? How so?"

"Because the crater must be blocked by rocks and lava."

"And what if it's extinct?"

"Extinct?"

"Yes. There are only about three hundred active volcanoes on the earth at this moment, but thousands more are extinct, as is Sneffels. It last erupted in 1219."

As I could find no quarrel with these seemingly well-founded and apt observations, I changed the subject:

"What does Scartaris mean, and what is its connec-tion with the calends of July?"

My uncle, who always had an answer for everything, thought a moment, then explained:

"Sneffels has several craters. Presumably Saknus-semm wanted to specify the one which leads to the center of the earth. Now, he must have observed that, as the calends of July approach, Scartaris, one of the peaks of Sneffels, casts its shadow as far as the mouth of the crater in question. It's all there, in black and white, in the parchment. If, like our alchemist, we climb to the summit of Sneffels, the meaning of his instructions will become clear."

"But Uncle, all the theories of science prove that it is impossible to get to the center of the earth. For one thing, the temperature rises one degree for every seventy feet you go down and, if you apply that principle to the earth's radius, the temperature down there must be over two million degrees Fahrenheit!

Any solid matter is turned into burning gas, and nothing can survive such intense heat. So I don't see how such a journey is possible."

This speech drew a mocking smile from the Professor.

"The truth is," he replied, "that no one knows what happens in the center of our planet. One scientist has shown that if the ambient temperature down there were two million degrees, the incandescent gases given off by the melted matter would produce such enormous energy that the earth's crust would be unable to withstand it; it would explode like an overheated boiler."

"That's just one man's opinion. Others may have different ideas!"

"That's possible, but other very eminent geologists have endorsed his theory. Also, don't you think it remarkable that the number of active volcanoes has been steadily diminishing ever since the world's creation? From this I conclude that, even if the earth's core was once very hot, it has since cooled down and will continue to do so."

"Uncle, may I point out that we are now moving into the realms of speculation?"

"All I'm saying is that I'm not the only scientist who thinks so. Do you remember when the famous English scientist, Humphry Davy, visited me in 1825?"

"Yes, I do!"

"When he visited Hamburg, we had many long discussions, particularly about the possible existence of a liquid core at the earth's center. We agreed that this would be out of the question, and no one since has provided evidence to the contrary."

"And why did you come to that conclusion?"

"Well, such a mass of liquid would be subject to the attraction of the moon, as the oceans are. Consequently, twice a day there would be internal tides which would put pressure on the earth's crust, producing periodic eruptions or earthquakes."

6. 'Why are we leaving so soon?'

I have to admit that my uncle's arguments were beginning to convince me and I decided to think them over in peace and quiet. After so much talking, I left my uncle's study in a daze. I felt in need of fresh air, and strolled down to the banks of the Elbe, stopping at the point where the ferry-steamer plies the river with its cargo of passengers. Some fate must have been guiding me for, just a few yards away, I saw Graüben, who had returned from her holiday, and was walking back home.

I called out to her and she turned around, startled. I ran to her side.

"Axel! You came to meet me!"

Then she must have noticed my worried expression, for she asked:

"What's wrong? You look as though something's on your mind."

I gave her the facts as briefly as I could. She became thoughtful. We turned and walked hand in hand toward the Professor's house.

"Axel!" she said at last, "I envy you going on such a wonderful journey!"

I stopped short in astonishment.

"I don't know whether you realize the dangers of such an enterprise!"

"Experience has shown that any adventure has its share of risks . . ."

"If I'm not mistaken, not only are you not trying to dissuade me but, on the contrary, you are encouraging me to go!"

I was put out and even a little ashamed. But Graüben added with a smile:

"Dear Axel! How I would love to go with you!"

"I shall never understand women! One minute you're timid, the next incredibly brave. It seems that reason doesn't come into your lives."

Night had fallen by the time we reached the house in Königsstrasse. I found my uncle in a highly excited state. Shouting, rushing about, he was bullying poor Martha, who was at her wits' end.

As soon as he saw me, he called:

"Axel! Come along! Your trunk isn't packed yet!"

"Are we going, then?" I stammered, taken aback by all this hustle and bustle.

"Of course we are! Instead of strolling around the town, you should have been here, getting your things ready. We leave the day after tomorrow, first thing in the morning!"

"Why are we leaving so soon, Uncle? It's another month before . . ."

"There's a boat that sails from Copenhagen to Reykjavik once a month and if we wait for the June sailing we may arrive too late to see Scartaris' shadow pointing out our crater. Time you got your bags packed!"

I took refuge in my room, where I spent a terrible night, troubled by dreadful nightmares.

The next morning Martha knocked on my door and told me that breakfast was ready and that Graüben wanted to talk to me.

"Ah! There you are!" said Graüben, as I walked into the dining room. "I'm glad to see you looking

My uncle was full of praise for my cleverness and I decided to try to change his mind about the journey while he was still in a good mood.

You asked me the meaning of the word "Yokul"...This is one of the best maps of Iceland currently available.

The island is dotted with volcanoes: they're all known as "Yokuls", which means "glaciers". At that latitude the eruptions happen under thick layers of ice, and that's why all the Icelandic volcanoes have that name.

What does "Sneffels" mean?

Sneffels is a 5,000 foot high mountain, one of the highest in Iceland. It's a volcano that's been extinct since 1219. If the crater gives access to the center of the earth, it will become world-famous!

As for the word "Scartaris", that refers to one of the peaks of Sneffels, which has several craters. To indicate which one leads to the center of the earth, Saknussemm has noted that, at the end of June, Scartaris' shadow touches the crater in question. The manuscript is very precise on that point.

I raised my objections: How could we penetrate a volcanic crater? What about the heat? My uncle managed to put my mind at rest. At this point, I decided to go for a walk and, by chance, met Graüben on her way home from holiday.

Do you mean that you're not going to try to dissuade me from taking part in this crazy expedition?

On the contrary! I'd love to go with you, but I'm afraid that I would only slow you down.

Later...

Why are we leaving so soon, Uncle? It's only May, so there's a month before

It isn't as easy as you think to get to Iceland, Axel!

There's a boat which does the Copenhagen-Reykjavik run once a month, and if we wait for the June sailing, we may arrive too late to see Scartaris' shadow pointing out our crater. But let's worry about getting to Copenhagen first, then we'll ask about the boats. Meanwhile, hurry up and pack your bags!

Scientific instruments, electrical apparatus, weapons and supplies were carried into the house. It was driving Martha to distraction!

Heavens above! Has my master gone mad? Where are you two going, Master Axel? To the cellar?

No, Martha, much lower, very much lower!

The next morning we took a carriage to the Altona station...

more relaxed than yesterday."

"More relaxed!" I exclaimed.

"I've had a long talk with your uncle," she went on. "He told me all about his plans, his hopes, and about this expedition. I'm sure it will be successful. Professor Lidenbrock's glory will be yours, too. When you come back you will be a grown man, a respected scientist, the future Professor of Mineralogy at the University . . ."

I had been dispirited before, but Graüben put new heart into me, and I became almost optimistic. However, I still could not believe that the expedition was really going to happen, so I went to ask my uncle.

"What?" he said. "Do you still have doubts? Go and pack your things, and be ready to leave in the morning!"

Without another word, I went up to my room. Graüben helped me to sort out my clothes and anything else I might need. She went about it calmly, as if we were going to a resort on the North Sea, instead of Iceland.

Throughout that day there was a continual procession of suppliers of scientific instruments, firearms and apparatus of all kinds which my uncle had ordered. Martha was tearing her hair, going from room to room, fighting her way through the boxes, trunks and parcels, muttering her opinion of her master as she went. Eventually, beside herself with frustration, she asked me:

"Is the Master mad?"

I nodded.

"Miss Graüben says that you're leaving too."

"That's right!"

"Where are you going?"

Looking down, I pointed towards the center of the earth.

"You're going to the cellar!" the good lady exclaimed.

"No Martha, further down, much further down!"

She went away, shaking her head, convinced that the nephew was as mad as the uncle.

The next morning I was awakened early, and went down to the dining room. My uncle was there before me and Graüben came in shortly afterward. We ate our breakfast in complete silence.

"Your trunk?" asked the Professor.

"It's ready!"

"Hurry and bring it down!"

My trunk and I reached the bottom of the stairs just as the carriage pulled up at the front door. We did not prolong our goodbyes. With her usual composure, Graüben kissed her guardian, but she could not keep

● A great mass of liquid can be subject to the attraction of the moon.

●● There's a boat that sails from Copenhagen to Reykjavik.

●●● She was convinced that the nephew was as mad as his uncle.

back a tear as her lips brushed my cheek.

"May God protect you, Axel!" she whispered in my ear. "I shall always be with you in my thoughts!"

7. He was talking loudly with a very tall and immensely strong man.

I clasped the girl I hoped to marry in my arms, then took my seat in the carriage. The two women stood at the door, waving a last goodbye. At the driver's command the horses set off at a gallop along the road to Altona, Hamburg's outer harbor. From there, the train took us to Kiel where we boarded the steamer *Ellenora,* bound for Copenhagen. There, while we waited for another boat—the *Valkyrie*—to take us to Iceland, my uncle made me climb right to the top of the Vor-Frelsers-Kirk belltower.

"Keep it up, Axel!" he cried, seeing that I was becoming dizzy. "You're going to have to get used to heights!"

Some days later, after a calm and uneventful crossing, we reached Reykjavik. As we sailed into Faxa Bay, my uncle, who had spent the whole voyage in his cabin suffering from seasickness, came up on deck. Taking me by the arm, he led me forward and pointed to a lofty, snow-covered mountain with two peaks.

"Sneffels!" he cried triumphantly. "Sneffels!"

And having yet again ordered me to keep our secret, my uncle clambered down into the boat which was to take us ashore.

As soon as we landed, he asked to be taken to one of his colleagues, a lecturer in natural sciences at Reykjavik University. Dr. Fridriksson spoke only Icelandic and Latin, so he used the latter when he spoke to me. I knew from the start that we were born to understand each other.

Pretending a merely casual interest, my uncle asked our host whether, by chance, he might have any information about a certain Arne Saknussemm whose name had cropped up in some conversation or other.

"Saknussemm!" exclaimed Fridriksson. "The great sixteenth-century scientist, naturalist, alchemist and explorer?"

"That's the man! I'd like to read some of his work."

"His work? But there are none of his books, either here or elsewhere!"

"How can that be?"

"Because all his published work was burned in Copenhagen in 1573, on the pretext that he was a heretic!"

"Ah! I see! That explains it!. . ."

My uncle had almost betrayed himself in his satisfaction with this information. Seeing the Professor's discomfiture, Fridriksson kindly dropped the subject

● He was a great 16th-century scientist, naturalist, alchemist and explorer.
●● His Icelandic colleague had decided not to accompany him on the expedition.
●●● Eider, the bird whose plumage is used in making eiderdowns.

and talked of other things. For my part, I now understood why Saknussemm, ostracized by society and forced to hide the nature of his discoveries, had concealed his secret in that fiendish cryptogram.

"I hope you will not leave Iceland without seeing some of its mineralogical wealth?" asked Fridriksson.

"By no means," my uncle replied.

"There are so many little-known glaciers, mountains, geysers and volcanoes on this island which deserve to be seen! Why, you need look no further than that mountain over there, on the horizon. That's Sneffels!"

"Sneffels?" said my uncle, indifferently.

"It is one of the most interesting of our volcanoes, yet the crater is rarely visited."

"Is it an extinct volcano?"

"Oh, yes, and has been for five hundred years and more."

"Since that's the case," the Professor continued, trying to appear only mildly interested, "I think I might like to begin my geological explorations with that . . . Seffel . . . what's it called?"

"Sneffels!" replied Dr. Fridriksson. "Yes, it should provide you with some interesting material. But you may have difficulty in reaching the Sneffels peninsula. There are no rowing-boats in Reykjavik. You will have to go by land, following the coastline. It's a long journey."

"Well, I'll see about finding a guide."

"Ah! I know of one."

"Is he a capable, reliable man?"

"Oh yes, and an excellent hunter into the bargain!"

This conversation ended, a few minutes later, with an exchange of compliments between the two scholars. My uncle was more than satisfied with the results of his inquiries and was relieved that his Icelandic colleague had decided not to accompany him on the planned expedition.

The next morning I was awakened by my uncle talking loudly in the next room. I got up, dressed, and went to join him. He was with a very tall man who, to judge by the width of his shoulders, was also immensely strong. He had a large, round face, and intelligent eyes. He was standing easily, his arms hanging loose, a perfect example of that calm, placid, unflappable type in whom English novelists delight. He did not gesture much, merely nodding his head occasionally to show agreement or shaking it slowly to show the opposite. However, from time to time, he let slip a word or two.

I learned from Dr. Fridriksson that this taciturn character was a hunter of eider, the bird whose

The train took us to Kiel, and the **Ellenora** to Copenhagen...

In Copenhagen my uncle took me up to the top of the Vor-Frelsers-Kirk belltower...

Keep it up, Axel, you must get used to heights, you know!

A little Danish schooner, the **Valkyrie,** took us aboard. My uncle suffered from seasickness during the voyage, which made him very ill-tempered...

He's been such a misery that the captain's thinking of charging us extra for the inconvenience. I knew that I should have stayed behind in Hamburg!

The **Valkyrie** dropped anchor in Faxa Bay, off Reykjavik...

Axel! Look! There's Sneffels!

But don't breathe a word! No one must know what we're doing here or we might be beaten to it!

We dined with Dr. Fridriksson, a lecturer in natural sciences, and my uncle expressed a passing interest in Arne Saknussemm.

Saknussemm was considered a heretic, and all his books were burned in 1573. None of them has survived.

Ah, I see!

My uncle was within a hair's breadth of giving himself away. At last I understood why Saknussemm had put his message in code: he had to keep his miraculous journey secret from the authorities.

To reach Sneffels by land you will need a guide. He will also be useful in the mineralogical study you are planning.

The next day our host sent us a guide. He was an eider hunter. He hunted the ducks for their down. Hans Bjelke was a capable, experienced man...

Hans agreed to take us to the village of Stapi and to stay with us until the end of the expedition.

Will he go with us as far as?

Yes, Axel, as far as the center of the earth. I haven't told him yet.

On June 16 we set off for Stapi. Our horses carried the provisions, equipment, weapons, gunpowder, not that we were going to meet any savages or wild beasts, of course!

plumage is used in making eiderdowns, and is the chief resource of Iceland.

This silent and phlegmatic man was called Hans Bjelke and was, in fact, the guide whom Dr. Fridriksson had so warmly recommended. His ways were in stark contrast to my uncle's, but they were soon getting on very well together, the one happy to accept what he was offered, the other content to offer what he was asked.

For a reasonable sum, Hans agreed to guide us to the village of Stapi, on the southern coast of the Sneffels peninsula, at the foot of the volcano. The distance by land was about one hundred and twenty-five miles, which was a good week's walk. Two horses would carry our luggage, and two more were needed for my uncle and me to ride. As was his custom, our guide would go on foot. It was agreed that he would be at my uncle's disposal for as long as the Professor had need of him.

Our departure was set for two days later and, once all the details had been settled, Hans took his leave.

"I must say, I like that man," my uncle declared. "But little does he know what the future has in store for him!"

"Do you mean that he's coming with us to . . ."

"Yes, Axel, to the center of the earth!"

We spent the hours before our departure in packing up our equipment and provisions.

On June 16, our preparations completed, Hans loaded up the packhorses, and we said our goodbyes to Dr. Fridriksson. My uncle thanked him warmly for his hospitality, then we climbed on to our horses and set off on the road to adventure.

CHAPTER 4

8. When science has spoken...

After crossing the Hvalfjord on a flat-bottomed ferryboat, we arrived, as planned, in the village of Gardär, where the houses clustered around a little church. It was our intention to spend the night here.

It should have been dark, but during June and July at the sixty-fifth parallel the sun never sets. All the same, it was bitterly cold, and we were glad of the hot meal which some peasants provided.

Six days later, we reached Stapi, a hamlet lying in the bed of a little fjord, tucked underneath the volcano. Our guide found us lodgings in the pastor's house.

Hans obtained the services of three sturdy Icelanders to carry our belongings. Once we reached the bottom of the crater, they would put down their burdens, collect their wages, and return to the village. My uncle took this opportunity to explain to our hunter that he was intending to explore the interior of the volcano. Hans merely nodded. To go there or anywhere else, to penetrate into the bowels of the earth, or climb the bleak mountains of his homeland — it was all the same to him. As for myself, I was haunted by an idea which was gradually turning into an obsession.

"So," I thought, "we are going to climb this confounded mountain, and explore every nook and cranny of the crater. Others have done the same and have lived to tell the tale. But there's more to it than that. If we happen to find a fissure, a path going down toward the center of the earth, and if that darned alchemist told the truth, it is highly likely that we shall get lost in some vast subterranean labyrinth. Now,

● The sun never sets during June and July at the sixty-fifth parallel.
●● If the steam is escaping through its normal routes, if it is not showing more activity and if the air doesn't become still and heavy.
●●● He built little pyramids with stones.

who can say for sure that Sneffels really is extinct? That it might not erupt at any minute? It wouldn't be the first time that a volcano has suddenly woken up after a long sleep! And if that happens, what will become of us?"

I was so obsessed with these thoughts that my dreams were full of erupting volcanoes. The prospect of being turned into lava was not particularly appealing! I was in such a torment, that I decided to mention the possibility to my uncle, in as offhand a manner as possible, as though I thought it highly unlikely.

So I told him of my fears, and waited for his reply. Instead of the derision I was expecting, my uncle answered calmly:

"Mm, I've been wondering about that, too! I've been turning it around in my head ever since we arrived here. You can be sure that I have no intention of putting our lives in danger."

"I never thought you would, Uncle!"

"If Dr. Fridriksson is to be believed, Sneffels has been dormant for over five hundred years. Now, eruptions are always preceded by well–documented phenomena. I have questioned the local people and carried out several tests, with negative results. I can therefore promise you, Axel, that we have nothing to fear from that direction."

This categorical assurance left me speechless. I spluttered:

"I believe you, Uncle!"

"Follow me, you can see for yourself!"

I did as he said. Striding along as usual, the Professor took a narrow path which led away from the sea and brought us to a vast expanse of volcanic debris. The ground was littered with huge rocks of solidified lava, basalt and granite. Here and there, steam hissed through deep cracks, and boiling water spurted out at regular intervals in clouds of vapor.

"You see that steam?" asked my uncle. "It proves that we need not fear a volcanic eruption."

"But I'd have thought it meant the opposite!"

My uncle smiled, and continued in a condescending tone:

"That's just where you're wrong, for although these vapors become twice as active as an eruption approaches, they disappear completely during the event, and do not recur until later. The molten lava and the compressed gases underground escape through the craters rather than through the fissures in the ground. So, if the steam is escaping through its normal routes as now, if it is not showing more activity, and if the air doesn't become still and heavy, one can be sure that the volcano is dormant."

We took a ferry across the fjord to the hamlet of Gardär, our first resting place.

I don't understand why it isn't dark yet!

You forget that we're close to the Arctic Circle. In June and July there's perpetual daylight in Iceland.

Some days later we reached Stapi, where we stayed with the local pastor. Before leaving the village, my uncle told Hans of his plans.

Hans didn't bat an eyelid. He doesn't seem to care whether we travel over or underground!

I, on the other hand, was scared...

Huh! Climbing to the top of Sneffels, exploring the crater, looking for a way down...even if Saknussemm was telling the truth, we're still likely to get lost in a subterranean maze...

Who can say that Sneffels is truly extinct? Perhaps it's about to erupt again! What would happen to us then? Every time I close my eyes I have nightmares...

That night I had an awful dream...

Oh! The volcano's shooting me into space!

I told my uncle about it the next day...

Don't worry! This steam proves that we have nothing to fear. It increases markedly just before an eruption, and disappears completely during the event. At that stage it all collects in the craters instead of coming out through these tiny cracks in the earth's crust.

As long as the vapors do not become more active, and as long as the air doesn't become still and heavy, you can be sure of one thing: there is no chance of an eruption taking place!

All the same...

Science has spoken. There is nothing more to say.

At nine o-clock the next morning, accompanied by Hans and three Icelanders who carried our equipment, we began our ascent of Sneffels. The insane adventure had begun!

I still had doubts:

"But . . ."

"That's enough!" he interrupted. "When science has spoken, we must bow to its arguments!"

There was nothing for it but to give in. My uncle's unanswerable arguments left me with no option. However, I still secretly hoped that, once we reached the bottom of the crater, we would be unable to go any further.

I had a terrible night. In my dreams I felt myself being shot into the air in the form of burning lava or an eruptive rock.

The next day, June 23, Hans was waiting for us with three porters, laden with provisions, tools, and instruments. Two metal-tipped sticks, two rifles, and two cartridge-belts had been set aside for us. With our own flasks, plus a leather bottle, we had enough water to last us a week.

After checking that nothing had been forgotten, Hans gave the signal for departure and, a few moments later, we left the cottages of Stapi behind us. At that time of year, Sneffels was still covered in a thick coat of icy snow. Led by our guide, we made our way in single file, along narrow paths where there was not enough room for two abreast. As befitted Professor Lidenbrock's nephew, I took great interest in the mineralogical curiosities which lined our route. The terrain was a mixture of spongy peat, alternating with pumice and other volcanic residues. Iceland is a relatively young island, and is, in effect, an accumulation of porous rocks. For all we knew, the island was still rising imperceptibly out of the sea. Long ago, a gigantic fault opened up diagonally across the island, letting out enormous quantities of magma which spread slowly, producing a wealth of minerals, such as feldspar, porphyry, granite and basalt.

Progress was becoming difficult. The slope was steeper now, and loose rocks and pebbles meant we had to watch where we stepped, to avoid dangerous falls. Hans walked on calmly. Sometimes he would disappear behind huge blocks, and he would be lost from sight for a moment. Often he would stop to build little pyramids with stones, to act as markers for our return journey, little knowing that we would never make use of them. From time to time he would give a whistle to show us which way to go.

Three hours' exhausting march brought us to the foot of the mountain. Our guide decided to call a halt, and told the porters to prepare a light meal. An hour later we were on our way again. The three Icelanders, as taciturn as Hans, took up their burdens and began the ascent of the volcano. An optical illusion, not

uncommon in mountainous landscapes, made the snow-capped summit seem very close; but we were still several hours' march away. Stones slithered underfoot, the rockface became sheer in places, and our iron-tipped sticks came in very useful. My uncle kept close to me, ready to catch me if I lost my balance. As for our companions, they were climbing steadily, with the agility of mountaineers.

By seven o'clock that evening we had covered two-thirds of the distance, and had reached a kind of platform on which the cone of the crater rested. We were now at the level of the perpetual snow-line, which is quite low in Iceland, due to the constant humidity of the climate. It was bitterly cold, with a strong, gusting wind. My uncle could see how tired I was and wanted us to rest. He made a sign to Hans who shook his head, pointing to the summit.

"Why?" asked my uncle.

"Mistour!" the guide explained.

My uncle then pointed down towards the plain. I saw a whirlwind of dust rising into the air, and being blown toward our mountainside. If it were to swerve our way, we would be swept up into its eddies. This was the phenomenon which the Icelanders called a "mistour".

We therefore moved upward as fast as we could. We reached the other side of the cone by a zigzag route. By the time the whirlwind hit the volcano we were already on the lee side. It had been a close shave! Eventually, at eleven o'clock, we breasted the summit of Sneffels.

As soon as I awoke the next morning, I went to admire the wonderful panorama which stretched out before me. Soon afterwards I was joined by Hans and my uncle.

Turning to the west, the Professor gestured toward a faint line on the horizon:

"Greenland!" he said excitedly.

"Greenland?" I exclaimed in bewilderment.

"Yes, Greenland! It is only about a hundred miles away, and during the thaw, polar bears land in Iceland, carried here on drifting icebergs. We are on the summit of Sneffels, and here are the two peaks the alchemist spoke of. I shall ask Hans the name of the one we're standing on."

Hans' reply to the question was:

"Scartaris!"

My uncle looked at me triumphantly:

"Down into the crater!" he cried.

It was a steep climb. Pieces of rock kept giving way and we had to watch our step...

From time to time Hans would gather some stones and build cairns to mark our route for the return journey, little knowing that we would never make use of them.

At about seven o'clock that evening we reached the perpetual snow-line. Just as we stopped to rest.

Mistour, mistour!

What is it?

The Icelandic word "mistour" refers to the clouds of dust and sand which are whipped up by the strong winds which come off the mountains. We'd better follow Hans' advice and take shelter!

Although we were dropping with fatigue, we carried on and eventually reached the summit of Sneffels where we pitched our tent.

The next morning Hans told us that we were on the peak of Sneffels called Scartaris.

There is no time to lose! Quickly! We must get down into the crater!

Sneffels' crater was in the form of an inverted cone, measuring about a mile across and about two thousand feet deep. It must have been an awe-inspiring sight when it was full of lava and molten rock!

It's like going down into a bottomless pit. He must be mad even to have considered this journey. We'll probably all be killed by falling rocks!

But it was too late to go back! Hans, who led us down, was following a course which took us in increasingly tighter circles. The descent grew steeper.

At about noon we reached the bottom. There we found three chimneys, each about one hundred feet across. They were once the escape routes for lava and gas during eruptions.

9. 'Look what's written on this rock!?'

The crater was shaped like an inverted cone and was about a mile across. I estimated its depth at two thousand feet, but the sides seemed to slope very gently, and the way down looked easy. Despite my fears, there was no going back. Completely unmoved, Hans took the lead and I followed him blindly. To begin with, he wound his way round the inside of the volcano in long ellipses. We threaded our way between huge rocks, our footholds often precarious. Some of the rocks toppled in our wake, bouncing down into the depths below. Hans moved forward very cautiously, prodding the ground with his stick to locate any crevices or fissures. At certain critical points we even had to rope ourselves together, like alpinists. By noon we had reached the bottom. When I looked up I could see the rim of the crater, framing a patch of sky. At the bottom of the crater were three chimneys, through which lava and sulfurous steam had once erupted. Each of these openings was one hundred feet wide, and I was too scared to lean over and look into the yawning chasms. My uncle, however, was running excitedly from one to the other, gesticulating and muttering. The Icelanders watched him in astonishment, doubtless convinced he was a lunatic.

All at once my uncle gave a shout. Thinking he must have lost his footing and tumbled into one of the chimneys, I ran toward the noise. But I need not have worried: my uncle was standing, ecstatic, in front of a large block of granite.

"Axel!" he shouted. "Come here! Come and see!"

I ran over to him.

"Look what's written on this rock!"

I was dumbfounded to see, at eye level, some signs which had been half worn away by time, engraved on the western face of the rock! There before my eyes was a series of runes, similar to those on the parchment.

"These runes are the ones for the name you decoded," declared the Professor. "Arne Saknussemm! Isn't it wonderful?"

I said nothing. I was now convinced that the path the Professor was taking would lead us to the center of the earth, and was overwhelmed by a dreadful premonition. When after a long time I at last looked up, I saw that only Hans and my uncle were there. The porters had put down their loads, and were already making their way back up to the summit. From there, they would return to Stapi by the same route we had taken that very morning. Thoroughly exhausted, and leaving our guide to pitch the tent, I settled down as best I could in the shelter of a rock, covered myself with a warm blanket, and fell into a

● It is a kind of whirlwind of dust.
●● They were a series of runes, similar to those on the handwritten parchment.
●●● The change in the moon can have some influence on the weather.

deep sleep.

As soon as I awoke the next morning, I could tell that the Professor was beside himself with frustration, and he was swearing like a trooper. I understood the reason and saw there was still hope of a reprieve, when I looked up into a grey sky, heavy with rain.

Of the three openings before us, only one, apparently, had been explored by Saknussemm. If we were to follow his instructions, we would know which one to choose by the indication in the cryptogram: Scartaris would cast its shadow on the edge of the right opening during the last days of June. Today was June 25. If the sky did not clear within a few days, we had wasted our time, and would have to return the following year.

On the 26th, sleet fell all day. Hans took advantage of any dry periods to build us a shelter out of blocks of lava and pumice stone. On Sunday 28 with a change in the moon came a change in the weather. The sun reappeared, spilling its rays into the crater. Every hillock, every basalt rock, cast its shadow on the ground. The largest of these shadows, that of Scartaris, moved around almost imperceptibly, shortening as the sun climbed in the sky. Fascinated, my uncle moved with the shadow. At noon precisely it brushed the central chimney. The Professor shouted joyously:

"That's it! It's there! Here is the path to the center of the earth!"

I looked at Hans who seemed to have understood, although his face showed no surprise.

"Forward!" roared my uncle, repeating his command in Icelandic.

We quickly packed our supplies, equipped ourselves with ropes, crampons and pitons and, at thirteen minutes past one, began our journey in earnest.

I was too scared to lean over and look inside. The professor was running from one chimney to another, talking to himself as he went. Hans and the three Icelanders were sitting on some stones, watching my uncle as he strode about.

Suddenly... Quickly, Axel! Come and see what I've found on the side of this rock!

It's Arne Saknussemm's name carved in Runic letters! Now will you believe me?

We sent the porters home and prepared for our first night in the crater. The next morning was grey and overcast. My uncle was in a raging temper...

If the sun doesn't shine there will be no shadows, and without Scartaris' shadow we cannot tell which of the three craters leads to the center of the earth!

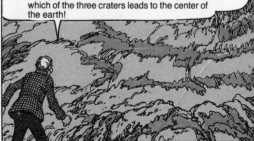

I began to think that luck was on my side. Today was June 25. If the sun didn't come out in the next six days, we would have to pack our bags and wait until the following year. But the sky cleared on June 28 and...

There it is! Scartaris' shadow! This is the chimney that will lead us to our destination!

I walked over to take a look, but was overcome by vertigo. A strong hand drew me away from the edge...

We divided our equipment into three bags, lowered a rope down the shaft and went down as far as the rope would take us. We would then retrieve the rope and keep repeating the operation until we reached the bottom.

Half an hour into this hair-raising descent...

We've pulled the rope down after us. Now for the next stage.

Watch out for falling rocks!

Whether this level dates from the Pliocene, the Miocene, the Eocene, the Cretaceous, the Jurassic, the Triassic or the Devonian periods, whether the rocks are old or new is the least of our worries, I'd thought! But look at him writing it all down!

The more I see of these volcanic rocks the more I come to think that Davy's theory is correct. We are right in the middle of the primordial stratum, in which the chemical phenomenon of metals catching fire on contact with air and water occurred! I absolutely reject the theory of central heat. In any case, we shall soon see!

CHAPTER 5

So far I had not dared to look down into the bottom-less pit which we were about to enter. But now the time had come. I would have been ashamed to hesitate when Hans was treating the challenge so calmly, and I cringed at the thought of being less brave than he. I therefore tried to seem enthusiastic. Looking up one last time at the patch of blue sky above my head, I thought of my dear Graüben and walked over to the central chimney. Leaning over a projecting rock, I took a quick look. A shiver ran down my spine and my hair stood on end. I felt so giddy that I would have fallen, had not Hans seen and pushed me back from the edge.

But even if I had only glanced down into the void, I had seen enough to register its shape. The side walls were almost perpendicular, but there was a series of projections which would make our descent easier. All we needed was a rope to hold on to as we made our way down; but how were we to retrieve it once we reached the bottom? My uncle had a simple solution to the problem. He uncoiled a length of rope about as thick as a thumb and four hundred feet long, dropped half of it down the chimney, looping the middle part over a projecting rock, and lowered the remainder down into the hole. Each of us could then go down, holding on to both halves of the rope, which was now secure. Once at the bottom, it would be a simple matter to pull on one end and bring the rope down behind us. We would repeat the operation as often as necessary until we reached the bottom.

10. A few mouthfuls of water mixed with gin, a biscuit... our breakfast!

Now, said my uncle, "we must divide our equip-ment up into three loads. We shall each carry one on our backs. Hans will take the tools and one-third of the provisions; you, Axel, your third and the weapons; and I shall take the remaining provisions and the instruments."

The Professor fastened the pack with the instruments on his back, Hans took the one with the tools, and I the weapons parcel. The descent began in the following order: first Hans, then my uncle, then me. Not giving myself time to think, I let myself slide down, clutching my metal-tipped stick for all I was worth. There was a deep silence, disturbed only by the sound of falling stones and gravel, dislodged by our nailed boots. The thought that the rope support above us might give way, casting me into the abyss, made me rigid with terror. Our rope seemed much too flimsy to take the weight of three heavily laden men. Fearing the worst, I tried to use the rope as little as possible, seeking out footholds and performing marvelous feats of balancing on the lava projections.

Whenever one of these slippery steps shook under Hans' feet, he would quietly warn us:

"Gif akt!"

"Look out!" my uncle would translate.

After half an hour of this exhausting descent, we reached a sort of narrow, slippery ledge, jutting out into the chimney.

Hans pulled on one end of the rope; the other came down, bringing with it a hail of stones which clattered down around us. I peered over the edge and found that the bottom was still invisible. The darkness stretched menacingly and infinitely below our feet.

Repeating the rope maneuver which had been so successful the first time, my uncle chose a rock, looped our rope over it, and we started down again. Half an hour later we were two hundred feet further down.

Three hours passed, and still we had not reached the bottom. When I looked up, I could see a little piece of sky through the top of the chimney, growing ever smaller as we continued our descent. The walls seemed to be sloping slightly toward the middle. It was gradually getting darker. We were still going down. I could now hear loose stones making a dull thud as they hit the ground, and I assumed we had not much farther to go. I had been counting the number of times we repeated the rope maneuver, so I had a rough idea how far down we were. According to my calculations we had taken ten and a half hours to reach a depth of some 2,800 feet. As I reached this conclusion, Hans called out:

"Halt!"

I stopped short, gripping the rope.

"We've reached the bottom, I presume," said my uncle, as his feet touched level ground.

● A rope to hold on to as they make their way down.
●● Axel calculated ten and half hours.
●●● He uses the barometer and the manometer for measuring air pressure.

I slipped down beside him.

"We have arrived, Axel!"

"Where?"

"At the bottom of the chimney!"

"What use is that, if there's no way out?"

"There is one. I think I can make out some kind of corridor slanting away to our right. But let's rest now. We'll take a look tomorrow."

Our guide lit a paraffin lamp and opened a bag of provisions. When we had finished our meal, we tried to find a sleeping-place where we would be sheltered from the falling stones and the water trickling down the walls. Lying on my back, I could see a star shining in the sky, far above us.

Eventually, tired out, I fell into a deep sleep.

It must have been about eight o'clock when a ray of daylight, finding its way to the bottom of the chimney, woke us up. It shed enough light to show us our surroundings.

"Well, Axel! I hope you slept soundly?" my uncle asked, rubbing his hands. "This certainly makes a change from our house in the Königsstrasse. There's no noise here, not even a whisper. Total silence!"

"You're right there, Uncle, but it's so quiet it's creepy!"

"Come now, my boy! If you're scared now, what will you be like when we're deep in the bowels of the earth?"

"What do you mean?"

"Simply that we've only reached the bottom of the island. This is sea-level."

"Are you sure?"

"Absolutely! That's the reading on our instruments! Look at the barometer!"

Sure enough, the mercury level read twenty-nine inches.

"You see," my uncle went on, "the air pressure here is still normal. From now on we shall have to use the manometer instead of the barometer as the air pressure will be greater than at sea-level."

"But won't the increasing pressure and rising temperature mean that things will get very uncomfortable?"

"We shall be going down slowly, in stages. That way, our lungs will gradually become used to breathing a denser atmosphere. It's the opposite problem from a mountaineer who gets less oxygen the higher he climbs. We may have too much. But we can't just stand here talking — there's no time to lose!"

A few mouthfuls of water mixed with gin, a biscuit and some dried meat made up our breakfast, and we had soon finished. My uncle took out his notebook to

write down his scientific observations. He consulted his various instruments and made meticulous notes of his readings from the thermometer, hygrometer and barometer.

When this was done, he cried enthusiastically:

"Axel! This is the moment we have been waiting for! We are about to penetrate the veritable depths of the earth!"

So saying, he connected the battery hanging round his neck to the light bulb in his hand. A bright light illuminated the bottom of the chimney and the entry to the gallery.

Hans connected his light, too. This ingenious use of electricity enabled us to dispel the darkness and follow in the footsteps of the great Saknussemm.

We each picked up our bundles and, in single file, headed into the corridor.

As far as we could tell, this tunnel had been the path along which the lava traveled during the last eruption, before flowing down the sides of the volcano. The walls were lined with solidified basalt and porphyry, which reflected and intensified the light from our lamps. The sight held me enthralled. It was as if the genii of the depths were lighting up their palace to welcome their visitors from the surface of the planet. I consulted the compass at regular intervals, and found that we were following a perfectly straight downward path. From time to time, my uncle would stop to take measurements, which he would enter in his notebook, but he always kept the results to himself.

At about eight o'clock, after an afternoon spent walking through slippery mud, the Professor called a halt. We had stopped on a dry stretch, where the ground was firm enough to sleep on.

Hans spread out some food on a block of lava and we ate heartily.

We then hung our lamps up on some protruding rocks, and saw that we were in a sort of cave. There was a slight draft. Where was it coming from? What was causing it? Exhausted after seven hours of almost continual walking, I did not try to answer my own questions. However, one thing was worrying me: I had just noticed that we had drunk half our water. My uncle was planning to fill our flasks from underground springs, but I had as yet seen none. I shared my fears with my uncle.

"Don't worry, Axel," he replied. "We shall soon have more than enough water for our needs."

"But when?"

"When we are no longer surrounded by this layer of lava."

There was no reason to disbelieve him, so I kept quiet and let him carry on entering his figures in his notebook.

A few minutes later he informed me that we were ten thousand feet below sea-level and that the temperature was a mere 15°C. I must have looked rather doubtful, for the Professor gave me a look that spoke volumes and replied sharply:

"You know I never make mistakes in my calculations! If I did, then figures wouldn't be figures any more!"

I did not have to be told twice.

The next day, June 30, at six o'clock in the morning, we continued our descent. We were still following the tunnel hollowed out by the burning lava. It was something like a natural ramp. The surface underfoot was firm, making for easy progress. We walked on steadily until noon, when Hans suddenly stopped at the intersection of two galleries, each as dark and narrow as the other. Which one to choose? That was the problem. My uncle did not want to seem indecisive and arbitrarily pointed to the one leading east. In any case, no amount of careful consideration would help in such a situation, for there were no clues as to which way to go. We might as well trust to luck.

This new tunnel sloped down more steeply, and its height was very variable. One minute the ceiling would be out of sight, the next it was so low that we had to bend double to move at all. It was becoming comfortably warm. I could not help thinking that Sneffels had once spewed lava and gas through this tunnel. I could imagine torrents of liquefied rocks, thrust ever onwards by the enormous pressure from the bowels of the earth.

"Let's hope," I thought, "that the old volcano doesn't take it into its head to start up again!"

There was no point telling my uncle what I was thinking. He would not have understood, and he was obsessed with the idea of going onwards and downwards, farther and farther towards what the Icelandic alchemist had called "the center of the earth".

At six o'clock that evening, after an easy day's walk, we had covered some six miles, but had only increased our depth by a quarter of a mile. After a quick meal, we withdrew to our makeshift beds and slept.

The next morning we continued our journey. We felt rested, fresh and ready for the next stage. The gallery sloped so gently, the ground was almost level. Before long I had the feeling that we were going

11. This tunnel is taking us towards the surface, not downwards!

● The walls were lined with solidified basalt and porphyry.
●● They just trusted to luck!

It took us ten and a half hours to descend three hundred yards to the bottom of the shaft.

Tomorrow morning we'll explore that gallery. But let's sleep now!

The next day...

I'm willing to bet that you haven't slept so well for ages! No noise from the outside world! Complete silence!

Yes! But this silence makes me uneasy!

The bottom of this shaft is only at sea-level so we have a long way to go. Keep your chin up, my boy! Look at the barometer. You'll find that I'm right...

We each picked up our bundles and in single file set off into the gallery with our electric lamps lighting the way.

One last look at the sky! I don't think I'll be seeing it again for a long time!

Lava from the eruption of 1219 lined the walls of the tunnel which was leading us southeast. We were traveling vertically rather than horizontally.

At the end of the day we settled down to a meal. I was worried about our low stocks of water...

We'll find some farther on. The water can't get through the lava on this section.

We are deeper than any man has ever been by about ten thousand feet. The temperature, however, doesn't seem to have increased: it's still 15°C! It should be 80°! That's probably explained by the fact that we're in an extinct volcano.

Yet another unexplained puzzle! The next morning, June 30, we set off again, but, six hours later...

Let's trust to luck and take the one pointing east!

Which tunnel should we choose?

I was overwhelmed by the beauty of this gallery...

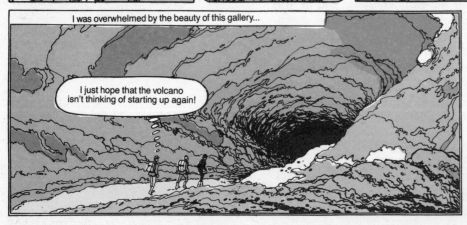

I just hope that the volcano isn't thinking of starting up again!

We traveled six miles southwards, but only descended a quarter of a mile. The next day I realized that, instead of going down, we were walking uphill!

If this carries on, with any luck we'll be back at the surface!

upwards rather than down. Puzzled by this development, I slowed down.

"What's wrong with you, Axel?" asked the Professor impatiently.

"Nothing in particular. I'm just exhausted, that's all!"

"But we only started three hours ago! This is an easy walk!"

"It is, but it's much harder than before."

"What do you mean? There's nothing easier than walking downhill!"

"Don't you mean uphill . . .?"

"Uphill? Are you mad?"

"You may not have noticed it, Uncle, but this tunnel is taking us towards the surface, not downwards!"

Dismissing my protests with a shake of his head, the Professor gave the signal to go on. His silence was revealing. He felt humiliated, and was keeping his feelings hidden, rather than admit he'd made a mistake.

I hoisted my pack higher on my back and walked on behind Hans and my uncle. Later in the morning I noticed a change in the tunnel walls. They were not reflecting our lamplight so powerfully. The lava had disappeared, and we were now surrounded by chalk and sandstone.

"Uncle!" I called, stopping in my tracks. "Look at these sandstones, limestones and schists!"

"Mm! And what do they imply, in your opinion?"

"That this level dates from the appearance of the first plants and animals on earth."

"Oh! Do you think so?"

"See for yourself!"

The Professor shone his light on the walls. Instead of the show of anger I was expecting, there was nothing: not a word. I had not gone a hundred yards before I suddenly found undeniable proof of my theory. Bending down, I picked up a perfectly preserved shell, which must have belonged to one of the trilobite species of marine creatures. The ground was littered with plant and animal remains, in varying stages of fossilization. I ran up to my uncle and showed him what I had found.

"Well! It's the shell of a crustacean of the trilobite species, that's all."

"But doesn't it lead you to any conclusions?"

"Of course! The same as yours! We have left the lava and granite level and are now surrounded by limestone and alluvial rock formations. I'm prepared to admit that I might be mistaken, but we cannot be sure until we reach the end of this gallery. So, let's get a move on!"

● He felt humiliated and was keeping his feelings hidden, rather than admit he made a mistake.

●● The water supplies would last only three more days, and the porous rock was not the place to find a spring.

"I'm sure you're right, Uncle, but I'd just like to point out that we've nearly run out of drinking water and we haven't come across any springs yet."

"Poor Axel," replied my uncle sympathetically, "I'm afraid that I'm not half as worried about it as you appear to be. The solution is simple. We'll just have to ration ourselves!"

CHAPTER 6

A nd ration ourselves we must, for our water
supplies would last only another three days, as I
found out at supper-time. And to add to my worries,
there was little chance of finding a spring in such a
porous rock system. The whole of the next day we
walked on along this seemingly endless gallery. Hardly
a word passed between my uncle and myself, and
Hans did not open his mouth once.

Magnificent marble seams lined the tunnel walls.
Some were a greeny blue, streaked with white veins,
others were a vivid red, or yellow with red blotches,
but all these marbles bore impressions made by primitive plants and animals. The rudimentary trilobites
had given way to traces of petrified fishes and reptiles
which would have enraptured any paleontologist. It
was plain that we were climbing up through the stages
in animal evolution of which man was the grand end
product, but my uncle did not seem to care.

The next day, after a ten-hour uneventful walk, I
suddenly noticed that the marbles, schists, limestone
and sandstone had been replaced by a dark, dull
substance. At a point where the tunnel narrowed, I
put my hand against the wall for support. It came
away black. We were walking into a coal seam.

"We're in a coal mine!" I shouted.

"A mine with no miners," observed my uncle.
"There is no indication whatsoever of human interven-
tion. But whether this coal has been worked or not, is
of no importance. It is supper-time!"

Hans quickly prepared some food. I ate hardly
anything, for my throat was too dry. Only our guide's
flask held any water, and that was barely half full.

12. All at once I smelled a strange odor.

By midday there was a change in the appearance of the gallery walls...

The lava's given way to chalk and sandstone...

Dismissing my comments with a shake of his head, the Professor gave the signal to go on.

Uncle, have you noticed how uneven these rocks are? We must be at the level of the first plants and animals on earth!

Huh!

We made a mistake when we chose this tunnel! We left the granite a long way back. We should turn around and go back to the point where the tunnel forked!

My uncle was too proud to admit that he had made a mistake, and we trudged on...

It's plain to see that we've left the gallery through which the erupting lava passed. This passage doesn't lead to the center of the earth. We should take more notice of the changes in the rocks: they will show us the right way to go.

I decided that if my calculations were correct, we should soon find some animal fossils...

Look, Uncle! This is the shell of a sea creature, a Trilobite. At that time the oceans were inhabited by more than fifteen hundred animal and vegetable species.

I admit that you're right: we have left the lava tunnel, but I am not prepared to say that I have made a mistake until we reach the end of this gallery.

Another day walking in the wrong direction and we're about to run out of water!

The next day we came to a very cramped section. I touched the wall and...

14

Uncle! We're in a coal mine!

A coal mine, eh? Well, it's a mine without miners!

The next day I could tell by the smell that the tunnel was full of firedamp, a combustible gas. Luckily we were using electricity for lighting, for just one spark could have produced a tremendous explosion...

We must get on! There is no time to lose!

After a long walk we came to a dead end: there was no way through!

Obviously this was not the route that Saknussemm took. We must go back! It's the only solution...

20

Providing we still have the strength, Uncle! We are almost out of water...

When we had finished our meal, my two companions laid out their beds and were soon asleep. I closed my eyes, longing for sleep to claim me, for I was utterly exhausted, but I lay awake all night.

The next morning we set off again and twenty minutes later we came to a vast cave. It was clear that it had not been hollowed out by human hand, for the walls were unsupported. This cavern was a hundred and fifty feet high and a hundred feet wide. The ceiling looked very unstable and I was terrified that it might collapse on us at any moment. A violent disturbance must have split apart the geological layers long ago, leaving in its wake this gigantic space. The history of this part of the Icelandic subterranean rock formation would have been an open book to a geologist. The beds of coal had been broken up, and were now separated by layers of compacted sandstone and clay, crushed by the upper strata.

During the epoch which preceded the Secondary Period, the earth was gradually covered by a thick cloak of vegetation, due to the favorable conditions of warmth and moisture. The earth's crust was still elastic at this stage and moved with the mass of liquid at its core. Giant depressions formed and cracks opened on the surface of the planet. Decaying plant life accumulated under the stretches of water which were formed by the condensation of the moisture in the air. As the centuries passed, these vegetable remains turned into peat, then, through the effects of gas and fermentation, they became pure minerals. This is how the coal seams, which were later to become a rich resource in the industrial world, were formed. These thoughts were running through my mind as my uncle shone his lamp on the cave walls. For once, geology seemed to be leaving him cold. He was walking on, silently. I noticed that the temperature was more or less the same as in the lava tunnel.

All at once I smelt a strange odor: I recognized it as firedamp, a combustible gas which had killed thousands of miners in the past. It would need just one spark for it to explode and kill us instantly. Fortunately, we were using electric light, so we were in no danger. This walk through the coal mine lasted until evening. The surface was perfectly horizontal and my uncle was finding it hard to conceal his frustration.

The darkness was so complete that we could see no further than twenty yards ahead. Our lights showed us the same relentlessly black walls. Suddenly, the Professor stopped, confronted by a solid wall which blocked the end of the tunnel. There was no way through, not even a crack in the wall which we might widen. That was most certainly that: we had come to a

● The long evolution of coal and the process until it becomes a rich resource in the industrial world.
●● The little quantity of water his uncle gave him.

dead end, and would have to go all the way back again!

"What a relief!" sighed my uncle. "At least we now know where we stand. This can't be Arne Saknussemm's route. Let's stop here for the night. Tomorrow we'll go back to the point where the tunnels forked."

"If our strength holds out that long," I replied.

"Why on earth shouldn't it?"

"Because, by tomorrow, there won't be even one drop of water left."

My uncle shot me a withering look and said, clipping his words:

"Is that a good enough reason for us to run out of courage too?"

I did not dare reply, and turned away.

We set off early the next morning. We must not dawdle, for we were five days' walk from the intersection. As I had warned, by the end of the day we had run out of water. The only liquid available was half a bottle of gin but, since it burned my throat, I went without. I was feeling very low and became increasingly tired. More than once I had to ask my uncle to stop so that I could rest. My uncle and Hans sat with their backs against the wall, trying to nibble at some biscuits. A mist fell before my eyes and I lapsed into semiconsciousness. After a while, I could feel someone lifting me up and a voice seemed to come from a distance:

"Poor Axel! What a state he's in!"

Opening my eyes, I saw the Professor bending over me, looking at me with such compassion and tenderness that I was deeply moved. I was not used to him showing me such affection.

"Drink up!" he said.

Taking the flask which was hanging at his side, he brought it to my lips and made me drink the small amount of water it contained.

"Oh, thank you, Uncle!" I murmured.

"Think nothing of it, my boy! I only did my duty."

That precious mouthful of water, which my uncle had been keeping for just such an emergency, gave me back a little strength.

"There's only one thing left to do," I said. "We must go back to the crater."

"Go back?" cried my uncle. "What are you saying? From where we are, we can only go forward!"

He was silent for a moment, then continued:

"So . . . that water didn't restore your courage and strength, then?"

"Courage . . .! What's the use?"

"Am I to understand that you want to call it a day?"

This time I fought back:

"What? You're going to see this mad scheme through?"

"Give up an expedition which has every chance of succeeding? Never! I'm not a man to run away at the first sign of trouble! I shall see it through to the end, nothing will make me turn back. I concede that we didn't find a spring in the corridor we chose, true. That was purely due to the nature of the rocks. But what makes you think that it will be the same in the other tunnel?"

I shook my head and was about to reply, but the Professor did not give me a chance:

"Listen, Axel. The only thing that stands in our way is the lack of water. This is what I suggest. If we don't find water within the next twenty–four hours, then we shall return to the surface. Did you know that Christopher Columbus had the same disagreement with his crew? He asked them to give him three days, and although the men were ill and frightened, they granted his request: it was thanks to that that he discovered America."

Impressed by my uncle's determination, I murmured, much against my will:

"So be it, Uncle, and may God help us! Let's go!"

Hans took the lead, as usual. The Professor was holding his lamp up close to the walls, examining their structure and composition. As we penetrated farther into the gallery, we could see the different layers which made up the primitive terrain more clearly. Never before had geologists had such ideal conditions for studying the internal structure of our planet. Through the green–tinged schists ran metallic threads of copper and manganese, spangled with traces of platinum or gold. The light from our lamps bounced off the thousand facets of the rocks, breaking up into a sparkling aurora and I sometimes felt as though I were inside an enormous diamond. At about six o'clock that evening, we left this fairyland. The walls became more somber, the mica was mixed more and more with feldspar and quartz to form the primordial rock which constitutes the foundations of the world — granite. We walked on, listening carefully for any sound of running water. I was so weak with thirst, my legs could scarcely carry me. The Professor plodded on with a strength born of despair. This was our last day, our last chance: if we didn't find water, he would be obliged to keep his word.

Suddenly, my legs collapsed under me. With a groan I fell to the ground.

My uncle ran back to me, stared for a long time with his arms folded, then muttered:

"It's all over now!"

● The light of the lamps bounced off the thousand facets of the rocks, breaking up into a sparkling aurora.
●● "Vatten" is the word for water.
●●● Simply following the route of the stream.

We awoke early the next morning and set off at a fast pace toward the point where the tunnel forked!

We were desperately thirsty. Even though we rationed the water and eked it out with gin, our flasks were almost empty. Eventually, on July 8, we reached the intersection.

Despite his gruff, impersonal manner, my uncle was very fond of me. He proved it by letting me have his last drop of water. I had collapsed from thirst.

Thank you, Uncle!

I can't go on. We must try to get back to the crater in Sneffels.

Never! I set myself a task and I intend to complete it, come what may!

Listen, Axel! Our only problem is lack of water. We'll walk down the western tunnel and if we don't find some water within the next twenty-four hours I promise that we'll turn back.

You only have a few hours left in which to bring about a change in our fortunes, Uncle!

We started to walk down the other tunnel. By eight o'clock that evening there was still no sign of water. My legs gave way and I fell to the ground. I heard my uncle say, before I lost consciousness...

It's all over now!

I don't know how long I was unconscious. When I came round, I saw...

Hans is abandoning us!

No, that's impossible! Hans would never do such a thing. He must have gone in search of...

Indeed, soon after...

Vatten!

Water! I'm convinced that he's found water!

We followed Hans down the gallery and, an hour later...

What's that muffled noise? It sounds like a train!

It's water, an underground stream, and it's quite close!

As he spoke I lost consciousness. When I came round, I saw that my two companions were asleep, rolled up in their rugs. The Professor's words still rang in my ears: "It's all over now!" They tolled the death knell of his hopes. As for me, I was so weak that I saw no hope of my returning to the surface. Nearly four miles of rock and earth lay between me and the outside world. I felt crushed, empty. A few hours passed. I dozed. Suddenly, the noise of someone moving broke through my drowsiness. Opening my eyes I saw Hans walking down the tunnel, lamp in hand.

What did it mean? Was he going to leave us to our fate? My uncle was asleep. I tried to shout, but no sound would come from my blistered lips. The sound of our guide's footsteps grew steadily fainter in the darkness.

Once the initial shock had passed, I realized that there was no reason to suspect a man who had so far behaved impeccably. What is more, he could not be abandoning us for, instead of turning back up the tunnel, he was going farther down it. For quite some time I dwelt on all the reasons which could have induced Hans to leave us behind. I entertained the most fantastic notions.

Eventually, about an hour later, I thought I could hear the sound of footsteps in the distance. Soon I knew I was right: Hans was coming back! First I saw a ray of light, then a beam, which grew larger as he approached. All at once, the guide was silhouetted in the darkness. He walked over to my uncle, put his hand on the sleeping man's shoulder, and gently shook him.

"What is it?" asked the Professor.

"Vatten!" the hunter replied.

Although I knew not one solitary word of Danish, there could be no mistaking the meaning of this one:

"Water! Water!" I croaked, beside myself with joy.

"Yes, it is! Water!" repeated my uncle.

Within a few minutes we were ready. Hans led us down the steeply sloping tunnel. We had been walking for an hour, going ever deeper, when I made out a muffled, continuous roar, as of water falling from a great height.

"This time I'm sure!" I cried.

"Your patience is rewarded, Axel!" smiled my uncle.

Nevertheless, although I tried the walls with my hand, there was no sign of moisture. Another hour passed. The sound was nearer, but there was no way of telling whether the river was flowing over our heads or somewhere below our feet. There was obviously a

13. A jet of water shot out of the hole.

thick granite wall between us: I was tormented by the fact that it was so close, yet unattainable.

When we reached a certain point, Hans stopped and put his ear to the wall. He moved to and fro, listening carefully, over a six-foot length of the wall until, suddenly, he mimed that he had found the right place and picked up his little pickaxe.

I could not stop myself from shouting for joy:

"Hans has saved us! He's saved our lives!"

Our guide was calmly getting on with his task. With light blows he steadily wore away the rock, gradually making an opening. My uncle, an impatient man at the best of times, wanted to hurry the process along. He was just about to join in with his pickaxe when we heard a hissing noise. A jet of water shot out of the hole and hit the opposing wall. Hans was almost knocked over by the force of it and yelped with pain. I soon found out why when I dipped my fingers in the water: the spring was boiling hot!

The Professor, in his usual phlegmatic way, said:

"Well! We'll just have to wait . . . it will soon cool down!"

Since the water was boiling, it gave off a lot of steam which soon filled the tunnel. A stream was forming and running into the ground a few yards away. I filled up my flask. I was so thirsty that I drank the water while it was still hot. It had a metallic taste.

"There's iron in it!" I cried.

"All the better for settling our stomachs!" my uncle replied.

"We mustn't waste it! We can't afford to run out again!"

"Well, there's nothing we can do about it, since we haven't anything which would block up the hole. In any case, the spring must be inexhaustible. If we let the stream follow its natural course it will guide us downwards and refresh us as we go."

"What a good idea, Uncle! I'm sure we'll find the right route if we follow the stream."

"You're obviously feeling better, my boy!" said the Professor with a smile.

"I am! In fact, I can't wait to get on!"

"Not so fast, Axel! First we must rest for a while."

Our thirst quenched, our spirits restored, we all slept peacefully.

The next morning, at about eight o'clock, we filled up our flasks and set off again. The gallery wound and twisted through the granite chambers like a maze. At intervals, my uncle looked at his compass to make sure that we were not straying too far off our original course. The tunnel sloped gently, and the stream burbled along lazily beside us, leaving small pools in

its wake. Its presence gave us confidence and its gentle murmur relieved the deadly silence.

B y Friday July 10 we calculated that we were about six miles underground. All at once, we found ourselves on the edge of a terrifying abyss. My uncle looked down it, holding his lamp out, and concluded gleefully:

"The descent is much easier than it looks. There are plenty of projecting rocks to which we can anchor our ropes."

Hans unpacked the ropes and we began our descent. As my uncle had predicted, it was much less harrowing than the chimney descent in the Sneffels crater. The shaft, or fault, had been formed by the contraction of the earth's crust as it cooled, and it was quite narrow. Soon we were going down in a spiral, following the line of projecting rocks. If melted rocks had once erupted up through the fault, I was surprised to see that they had left no trace.

Concerned that we might slip if we grew too tired, we stopped to rest every fifteen minutes. We would sit down on a rock, with our backs to the wall. My uncle made an hourly record of the compass, chronometer, manometer and thermometer readings, to calculate exactly where we were. The stream which Hans had freed from its rock prison now became a cascade, so that we only had to stretch out to refill our flasks. Nevertheless, from what we could hear, it sounded as though our stream took up a more normal course lower down. In fact the shaft was getting narrower, like a funnel.

After several days' descent the almost sheer angle of the shaft eased off to about forty-five degrees, heading south–east. From that point the going was much easier. The stream was still our faithful guide.

On July 15, when we stopped for a rest, my uncle asked me straight out:

"Do you know how deep we are?"

"I have no idea!"

"We are eighteen miles down and one hundred and twenty-five miles from Sneffels."

"If your calculations are correct, we must be directly underneath the sea!" I cried.

"Is that so?"

"We can easily check," I replied.

Referring to my compass, I took some measurements from the map.

"I was right, Uncle! We have passed Cape Portland and your hundred and twenty-five miles mean that we're right under the ocean."

14. 'Perish your calculations!' answered my uncle angrily.

Hans eventually located the point where the noise was loudest...

We're saved!

Hans, you're a miracle-worker! You've saved our lives!

After an hour's work...

AAAGH!

The water was boiling, and we had to wait for it to cool down...

It tastes of metal!

Then it's excellent for the digestion! This is our own private spa!

Instead of plugging the hole, I suggest that we let the stream run its course ahead of us; that way it will show us which way to go and we'll have a guaranteed source of drinking water whenever we need it.

We awoke the next day feeling refreshed, and carried on down the gallery. On Friday, July 10, when we were about six miles below sealevel, we came to a shaft...

Well I never!

This is what the geologists call a fault. It's caused by the contraction of the rocks as they cool. It's strange that there are no eruptive rocks here. Hans! The ropes!

July 11 and 12 were taken up in the descent...

On July 13 our angle of descent decreased, and two days later we were eighteen miles below the surface, somewhere under the Atlantic.

We're under the sea; we've gone past Cape Portland!

There's nothing unusual in that. Many coal mines run under the sea!

We were going deeper and deeper and, on July 18, we came out into a large grotto.

Tomorrow will be a rest day, Hans.

After breakfast next morning...

The theory that temperature increases in relation to depth has been disproved. Humphry Davy was right. What d'you say, eh, Axel?

Nothing, Uncle!

"There's nothing unusual in that, Axel. Some English coal mines run under the sea."

The Professor may well have seen our situation as perfectly normal, but the thought that a vast mass of perpetually moving water lay somewhere overhead made me deeply uneasy. But I had to get used to the idea, for our corridor, sometimes wide, sometimes narrow, straight then winding, but heading definitely south–eastwards, was taking us ever deeper. Four days later we came to a huge cavern. We decided to rest here for twenty–four hours.

I awoke very early the next morning. I had become used to living in the dark, and had to some extent lost track of time. Contrary to what I had feared, I had quickly adapted to our underground life. The cavern formed a vast hall, with our faithful little stream running over its floor.

After breakfast, my uncle got down to business:

"Now, Axel, I am going to calculate our precise position. I want to be able to draw a map of our expedition when we return home."

"That will be very interesting, Uncle."

"Let's go over the situation: we are south–east of Iceland, some two hundred and thirteen miles from Sneffels. I would estimate that we are at a depth of forty–eight miles . . ."

"Good Heavens!" I exclaimed. "But don't the scientists believe that that is the lower limit of the earth's crust?"

"Maybe . . ."

"But, if that's the case, the temperature should be 1500°C!"

"You were right to say 'should'. Theories and facts are not always the same, my boy!"

"Obviously not, but I'm still rather surprised."

"The scientists seem to have miscalculated by 1,472.4°, from which we can deduce that the increase in temperature is not proportionate to the depth. In fact, this was Humphry Davy's belief and I'm glad I listened to him. What do you say to that?"

"Nothing, Uncle, nothing!"

In truth there were many things I could have said. I did not accept Davy's theory, being a firm supporter of the central heat hypothesis. Rocks are poor heat conductors, from which it follows that they are good insulators and the heat would be trapped beneath them. But I decided not to start an argument, but appear to take my uncle's word as gospel.

"I'm sure your calculations are right, Uncle," I said. "May I tell you what conclusions I draw from them? At our present position, in other words the latitude of Iceland, the earth's radius measures approximately

4,750 miles. Well, so far we have covered forty-eight of them . . ."

"That's correct!"

"And to reach this depth we have had to travel a diagonal distance of 213 miles, is that not so?"

"It is!"

"And it took us twenty days to do it!"

"Precisely!"

"And if we maintain the same time-distance ratio it will take us two thousand days, or about five and a half years, to reach the center of the earth . . . providing, that is, that we find the way!"

"Perish your calculations!" cried my uncle angrily. "They're based on pure theory. And who says that this corridor doesn't lead directly to the center of the earth? What we are doing now, someone else did several centuries before us. Where he succeeded, I shall succeed too!"

"I certainly hope so. But I'm entitled to have doubts . . ."

"Let's leave it there, Axel. Instead of getting hot under the collar with your theories, you would do better to look at the manometer. What does it say?"

"There's a lot of pressure."

"Good. You see, by going down slowly, in stages, our bodies have adapted perfectly."

"Apart from an occasional earache . . ."

"I'm sure you'll agree that's a small price to pay. Anyway, you can easily get rid of it by swallowing."

More determined than ever not to contradict my uncle, I changed the subject:

"Have you noticed how the increased pressure makes sound travel much faster than on the surface?"

"I have. A deaf man would be able to hear down here!"

"But, presumably, the air density will increase as we go lower?"

"Yes, by virtue of a little known law, for weight decreases with depth. In theory, there is total weightlessness at the center of the earth."

"So the air will end up by having the same density as water?"

"That's right, under a pressure of 710 atmospheres."

"And lower down?"

"Lower down it will increase even further."

"Then how will we be able to continue our descent?"

"Why, that's easy! We'll fill our pockets with stones!"

"My word, Uncle, you have an answer for everything!"

I did not dare press the matter further, in case I

● They were getting tired and were afraid of slipping.
●● They had been walking for twenty days.
●●● They filled their pockets with stones to be able to descend.

angered the Professor. My uncle would have used Arne Saknussemm as a reply to all my arguments, not that his precedent bore any weight with me for, even if he really had traveled this way before us, he would not, at that stage in scientific history, have had sufficiently advanced techniques for calculating the exact center of the earth.

I kept my own counsel, and determined to act like an Englishman and wait for events to take their course.

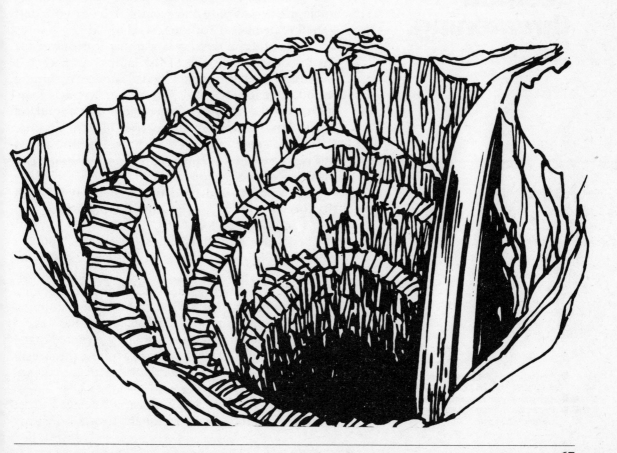

CHAPTER 7

15. The silence all around me seemed threatening.

For a few days, steeper, and sometimes almost vertical, slopes took us ever deeper underground. We made steady progress, each day taking us four or five miles nearer the center. During the two weeks following my long conversation with my uncle, there was only one event worthy of note, but I shall remember it for the rest of my life.

On that fateful day I was walking in front of the Professor, carrying one of the lamps. As I went, I examined the various rock beds. Suddenly, turning round, I realized that I was alone. Retracing my steps, I went back up the corridor but found no sign of my companions. I carried on for another fifteen or twenty minutes, with no result. I called out but received no reply, apart from a distant echo of my own voice.

I felt uneasy, and tried to reassure myself with the thought that there was only the one tunnel and that I could not be lost.

The silence all around me seemed threatening. I called out again, but there was no answer. Doubts plagued me: was I really in front of my companions? Was I sure my uncle and Hans were behind me? Of course, I could remember Hans stopping briefly to adjust the straps on his load. "Besides," I thought, "there is one sure way to guarantee that I won't stray off the right path: if I follow the stream back up, I can't avoid bumping in to my companions."

This plan gave me new heart and I decided to set off without delay. First, I thought I would rinse my

● If Axel follows the stream back up, he won't stray off the right path.
●● Axel must have knocked it on a rock.
●●● By calculations taking account of the speed of the light.

As the lava that flowed through this gallery cooled and solidified it formed heat-proof barriers. That's why the temperature is not higher and why we are still comfortable...

According to my calculations, Uncle, it will take us two thousand days to reach the center of the earth!

Hrumph!

If we continue to go down forty-eight miles for every two hundred and thirteen horizontal miles, in a south easterly direction, the odds are that we won't have found the center by the time we get back to the surface!

Hrumph!

Also...

What makes you think that this gallery doesn't lead straight to our destination? What Arne Saknussemm has done I shall do also! I shall not give up!

But distance isn't our only problem. Isn't it true that, as we go deeper and deeper, the air we are breathing will eventually become as dense as water because of the increase in weightlessness?

Certainly. But the pressure has to reach seven hundred and ten atmospheres before that happens.

15-

In that case, how can we keep on going down?

By filling our pockets with stones, my dear boy!

Sure enough, my uncle had an answer for everything!

The next two weeks were relatively uneventful. We continued our downward journey. We were lucky in having an experienced and careful man as our guide. On August 7...

These layers of granite are very interesting indeed...

Our continual descent has brought us to a depth of seventy-five miles; above our heads are seventy-five miles of rock, ocean, continents and towns and we're now five hundred miles from Iceland.

15/

When I looked round, I suddenly realized that I was alone...

Hans! Uncle! Hello!

No reply! Just an oppressive silence!

I was very worried and decided to retrace my steps, but, after walking for half an hour, I had still not found them...

They must be along here somewhere. I'll just have to keep going. There's only the one gallery. So all I have to do is to follow the stream, and I'll find them.

face, and I squatted down to scoop up some water in my hand. To my horror I felt rough, dry granite beneath my fingers! The stream had vanished!

I felt defeated. The prospect of never being able to escape from this labyrinth, of wandering aimlessly around looking for a way out, turned me cold. How could I possibly have left the course of the stream? All at once, I realized the hopelessness of my situation. At some stage, without even noticing, I must have turned off into a secondary tunnel and left the main gallery. But why hadn't the other two called out to warn me when they came to the junction? It was all beyond me.

Forcing down my fears, I tried to think. Images flashed through my mind: the house in the Königsstrasse, my beloved Graüben, Iceland, Dr. Fridriksson, Sneffels . . . I found myself sighing:

"Oh, Uncle! Why did I agree to come with you?"

They were the only words I could say against him, for I knew that the two men must be searching frantically for me. I decided to rest for a moment and check the supplies in my haversack. The results were encouraging: I had enough food and water for three days. But should I go downwards, or back up towards the crater? I plumped for the latter and set off. The going was steep and slippery, and I was glad of my iron-tipped stick. I made good progress during the next half hour, meeting with no major obstacles. I looked out for any distinguishing features I had noticed on my way down, but I soon had to face the facts: this gallery could not bring me back to the intersection, for it came to a dead end. Before me stood a granite wall, blocking the tunnel completely.

Any hope I had left drained from me. Weak and helpless I shouted, roared . . . but even the echoes had deserted me. The final blow was that my lamp seemed to be going out. I must have knocked it on a rock, and the light was flickering more and more feebly. I was terrified that it would stop working, plunging me into a darkness from which I would never come out alive.

There was one last gleam of light, then I was alone in the black depths. I felt I was going crazy. With my arms outstretched, I tried to feel my way along, stumbling, half-running downwards. I was bouncing, spinning off the rock walls. Suddenly I tripped and fell headlong on the ground. I picked myself up gingerly. My head had collided with a jutting rock and blood was streaming down my face.

I staggered on, blindly, but after several hours I dropped exhausted to the floor and lost consciousness.

When I came back to life I cried out with pain. I felt as though someone had beaten me to within an inch of my life. With great difficulty I managed to prop myself up against the wall. I thought I was going to pass out again when I heard a loud noise: it was like a thunderclap rolling round the subterranean tunnels. Where did it come from? What phenomenon had caused it? I listened again, placing my ear to the wall. I could hear faint sounds: they seemed like distant voices. "Am I imagining things?" I wondered.

I concentrated hard, and distinctly heard a murmuring, a kind of whispering; vague, incomprehensible words. My uncle and Hans could not be far away. If I could hear them, they must be able to hear me . . . .

I began to shout:

"I'm here! Help!"

But there was no reply.

Using the rock wall as a sounding-board, I tried to find a position in which I could pick up their voices. As far as I could tell, the sounds were coming from somewhere in my tunnel and seemed very close, due to some peculiar acoustic effect.

Fifteen minutes passed. Suddenly I heard my name called . . . . Yes, it was definitely my uncle's voice!

"Axel! Axel! Speak if you can hear me!"

"I can hear you, Uncle!" I shouted.

"Where are you?"

"Lost, in pitch blackness!"

"And the stream?"

"It's disappeared!"

"Don't worry, Axel, we're coming! Don't talk, just listen. We looked for you everywhere, up and down the main gallery. To give you a better chance of hearing us we even fired our rifles. But keep your chin up! We'll find you!"

"But where are you? How far away?"

"I'll find out. Listen carefully. I'm going to call out your name, and you must reply as soon as you hear me. Ready?"

I put my ear to the wall and did as my uncle asked.

"I shall just do some quick calculations. There was a gap of forty seconds between my call and your reply.

16. 'Start walking! You'll soon be back with us!'

I knelt down in the darkness to rinse my face, and felt only the rough, dry rock...

I don't understand it, I'm sure the stream was running alongside me!

I was as good as buried alive, destined to die of hunger and thirst. How could I get out? Which way should I go?

Oh, Uncle!

They were the only words of reproach that passed my lips. The Professor must be frantic with worry and I put myself in his place...

I must keep going upwards, sooner or later I'll reach the point where the tunnel forks and I'll find the stream which will lead me back to the crater...

I wandered around for a long time in the darkness, thinking of the people I might never see again...

Then I panicked, and began to run, crashing into the walls until I fell to the ground, exhausted.

I think I can hear voices!

Axel!

Through some strange acoustic effect I could clearly hear words and noises from a long way off...

I must move away from the wall if I want them to hear me.

Uncle!

They heard, and we held a shouted conversation. My uncle was making some complicated calculations...

Forty seconds elapsed between my question and your reply, so sound is taking twenty seconds to reach us, which means you are approximately four miles away. Keep your chin up, Axel. We'll be together again soon.

Following my uncle's instructions, I carried on downwards but, all of a sudden, the ground disappeared, my head hit a rock, and I passed out.

Now, taking account of the speed of sound, that makes approximately four miles."

"As much as that!"

"You can do it, Axel!"

"But should I go up or down?"

"Down, definitely, because we're in a cave with several galleries leading into it. Just head for our voices. The tunnel you are in must come out into this cavern. Start walking, Axel! You'll soon be back with us!"

Since I could hear my uncle's voice so clearly, it seemed plain that there was no obstacle between us. I felt my way along, dragging myself rather than walking. However, the slope was quite steep and soon I was able to let myself slide down the tunnel. I went faster and faster until the ground suddenly disappeared from under my feet. Feeling myself falling through space, I tried to latch on to some kind of handhold, but my head hit a rock and I lost consciousness.

When I came to, I was in semi-darkness, lying on some blankets. My uncle was standing beside me, looking concerned.

"He's alive! He's alive!" he shouted as I opened my eyes.

Hans hurried over. He saw my uncle holding my hand and smiled with relief.

"God dag!" he said.

"Good day, Hans!" I replied. "And now, Uncle, tell me where we are, and what time it is . . . ."

"We'll leave that until tomorrow, Axel! Rest for now! You are still very weak. I've looked at that cut on your head and it's not too serious."

"But at least tell me what day, what time it is!"

"It's eleven o'clock at night and today is Sunday, August 9."

When I awoke the next morning I looked around me. I was in a large grotto, decorated with magnificent stalagmites. There was a layer of fine sand on the ground. The darkness was broken by a faint light coming from a narrow opening. I could also hear a rhythmic noise, almost like the murmur of waves breaking on the shore.

I wondered whether I might still be asleep and dreaming, but there was no doubt that I was wide awake and that my eyes and ears were not mistaken.

"It must be a ray of daylight," I thought, "which means that we are back on the surface. Has my uncle really abandoned the expedition? Or did he reach his

● It was like the murmur of waves breaking on a shore.
●● After his fall—he hit his head—Axel imagined that he was back on the surface!
●●● A huge expanse of water, like a sea: the Lidenbrock Sea!

objective without my knowing?"

As I was wondering, the Professor came in.

"Good morning, Axel!" he cried heartily. "It looks as though your long sleep has done you good."

"It has!" I replied, standing up.

"Hans and I took turns in watching over you."

"I could eat a horse, let alone the breakfast which I'm sure Hans has prepared for me."

"You can thank him, my boy, because he looked after you, he put some secret Icelandic ointment on your wounds. It's marvelous stuff — they've healed up like magic."

Our guide, who was only waiting to be asked, came forward with some food, which I wolfed down while bombarding my uncle with questions.

I learned that my fall had caused part of the wall to collapse. I had been carried along with the avalanche and had slid fairly harmlessly down the steep slope, surrounded by a torrent of rocks, the smallest of which would have been enough to crush me.

"You were in a sorry state when we got you out," explained my uncle. "I still can't understand why you weren't killed. But I swear that from now on we shall stick together . . . next time we might not find you again!"

"Stick together?" I queried. "But why, Uncle? Isn't the expedition over?"

I must have looked utterly amazed, for my uncle replied:

"What's the matter, Axel?"

"I should like to ask you a question."

"Ask away!"

"Are you sure I'm all right?"

"How do you mean?"

"I haven't broken anything?"

"Of course not!"

"What about my head?"

"Well, apart from some bruises and minor cuts, it's all there, sitting firmly on your shoulders."

"But, Uncle, I think my brain is affected . . ."

"Your brain!"

"Yes! I'm imagining that we're back on the surface!"

"On the surface? Far from it!"

"Then there must be something wrong with me! I can see the daylight and hear the sea and the wind."

"Ah! Is that what's worrying you?"

"Can you explain it to me?"

"I can't explain anything, because it's inexplicable. Once again you will see that geologists still have a lot to learn."

I jumped to my feet:

"Let's go outside!"

"No, Axel, not yet! The fresh air might not be good for you, and your eyes aren't used to the light yet."

"Fresh air?"

"Yes, the wind is quite strong. I don't want you out in it before you're ready."

"But I feel perfectly well . . . honestly!"

"Maybe, but you might still have a relapse, and I don't mind saying that that could be very awkward. We may have a long crossing ahead."

Feeling more and more confused I spluttered:

"A crossing? . . ."

"Yes, we set sail tomorrow."

I couldn't contain myself any longer:

"Set sail? But to do that we need a river, a lake, an ocean!"

I was so agitated that my uncle let me have my way. I dressed quickly, and ran towards the opening.

To begin with I saw nothing, for it took my eyes several minutes to adapt after so long underground. When I looked again, I was flabbergasted:

"The sea!" I exclaimed.

"Yes," replied the Professor, "the Lidenbrock Sea! After all, I don't think anyone would dispute my claim to having discovered it and my right to name it!"

17. Like in the natural history museum!

And there it was, a huge expanse of water, stretching out of sight. The gentle waves were breaking on to the fine golden sand of the deeply indented coastline. Despite the beauty of this seascape, I could not help feeling uneasy. Lofty mountains extended out into the sea in spurs and promontories, eaten away by the surf, and fading into this unknown, eerie sea. It looked unreal. A strange brightness, neither sunshine nor moonlight, picked out every detail. None of the cliffs cast a long shadow; the light resembled that of an aurora borealis, a cosmic phenomenon shedding a diffused light over everything. It was white, cruel, and I noticed that it held no warmth. Around us everything seemed petrified. As for the sky, if such a name can be given to the vault overhead, it contained large masses of vapor which, as a result of condensation, would occasionally release torrents of rain.

When I came round...

He's alive! You're all right, Axel!

God dag!

Where are we, Uncle? What day is it? What's the time?

We'll tell you about it tomorrow; sleep now. Today is Sunday, August 9.

When I awoke the next morning...

A cave, sand everywhere. I can see daylight through that narrow opening!

What's that strange sound? It's like waves breaking on the shore. And, there's a wind blowing, are we back on the surface? Has my uncle changed his mind and given up?

I stumbled over to the opening...

No Axel, you're still too weak. Go back and rest. The crossing may be long and tiring...

What crossing?

Rest while you can. We shall set sail tomorrow!

Set sail? What are you talking about? There's no sea, lake or river that I know of here! And we can't set sail without a boat! Let me go out and see!

He agreed.

What a blinding light! My eyes are used to the darkness, I can't see...

After a while I could make out a massive expanse of water, stretching away to the horizon. It was a fantastic and wonderfully unreal sight!

The sea!

You should say the Lidenbrock Sea! No one will challenge my claim to be the first to cross it, so it is only right that it should bear my name!

Dumbfounded, I gazed out uncomprehending at this magnificent panorama. I looked, I admired, with a mixture of astonishment and fear.

My uncle, who was already accustomed to the sight, no longer wondered at it. After allowing me time to satisfy my curiosity he came up to me:

"Do you feel strong enough for a walk?" he asked.

"Of course, I'd love to."

"Take my arm then, and we'll go down to the shore. We'll walk along it a little way."

On our left were steep rocks, piled one on top of another in fantastic heaps. Streams of water cascaded over them, some hot and steaming, others cold, tumbling headlong to the sea. The stream which had led us through the dark labyrinth and which had brought us to this place was certainly one of them, but we could not tell which. I offered it a silent prayer of thanks and sighed:

"We shall miss our stream . . ."

"Bah!" replied the Professor. "It could have been any of them, it wouldn't have mattered!"

Looking round I saw, some five hundred yards away, a dense forest of trees. They were not particularly tall, but their tops were shaped like umbrellas with clear, almost geometrical outlines, and the wind did not seem to disturb them. They looked like petrified trees.

Intrigued and unable to identify them, I hurried towards the forest. When I reached it I cried in astonishment:

"I don't believe it! They look like giant mushrooms!"

"And so they are," said my uncle. "They are a giant species which is not found on the surface of the earth."

The mushrooms were thirty or forty feet high, with heads almost as wide. There were thousands of them, growing close together, and it was almost totally dark beneath these domes, crowded as closely together as the round roofs of an African village. But these strange trees were not the only form of vegetation. Farther along the shore stood groups of trees which I had no difficulty in recognizing, as they were related to our everyday species. The main difference was that these were gigantic. I saw lycopodiums, giant sigillarias, tree–ferns, lepidodendrons with cylindrical stems, ending in long

● A sort of giant mushroom which is not found on the surface of the earth.
●● In the polar regions, near the seventieth parallel.

leaves bristling with spines, like those on a cactus.

"This is unique, incredible!" the Professor exclaimed. "It is the flora of the Secondary Period of earth. These plants are the ancestors of the lowly plants in our gardens. A botanist would be in seventh heaven here. See, Axel, how wonderful it is! Have you noticed this dust underfoot, the bones scattered round about?"

"I think I've seen some like them in the natural history museums. They are the remains of animals who lived in the Tertiary Period on the shores of this subterranean sea. Wait a minute . . . I can see some complete skeletons! How did these animals survive so far down under the earth's crust?"

"At a certain stage, the elastic crust was subjected to violent movements, both up and down and sideways. These caused upheavals and subsidence, and some of the alluvial soil was carried to the bottom of the chasms."

"But, Uncle, if antediluvian animals lived here thousands of years ago, why shouldn't one of these creatures still be alive somewhere in the forests or behind those rocks?"

With this thought, I looked fearfully towards the mountains on the horizon, but no living creature stirred on those deserted shores. We were the only moving bodies in this still, apparently limitless universe. After an hour spent exploring the small beaches, I returned with some relief to the grotto.

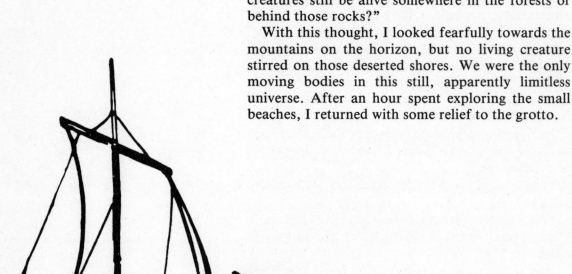

CHAPTER 8

The next morning I woke up feeling completely recovered. Being careful not to wake the others I went down to the shore of this strange sea and immersed myself joyously in its clear, cool water.

When I returned I found my companions eating breakfast.

"Uncle," I asked, "have you any idea where we are? Are the instruments any help in establishing our position?"

"Horizontally, we are 875 miles from Iceland."

"As far as that?"

"I'm sure I'm not mistaken. My measurements are accurate."

"And are we still traveling south-east?"

"Yes, with a deviation of 19 degrees and 42 minutes, as on earth. There is, however, a strange phenomenon to which I am paying particular attention."

"What's that?"

"The magnetic needle, instead of dipping towards the pole as it does in the northern hemisphere, is tending to point slightly upwards. I deduce that if we were to go towards the polar regions, near the seventieth parallel where, so James Ross says, the magnetic pole is situated, we would see the needle point straight up."

"And at what depth are we in relation to sea-level?"

"Eighty-eight miles, which means that the Scottish Highlands are directly above us," the Professor replied. "I admit that they're a heavy load to bear, but don't worry, their foundations are solid, the ceiling isn't about to collapse!"

"Very funny, Uncle! I'm not scared of the roof caving in on us, but I should like to know your plans. Are you going to head for the surface, or do you want

18. Crossing the Lidenbrock Sea on a raft.

Imagine! A cavern so enormous that it contains an ocean! But that light! Where is it coming from?

It's a stark white light, electrical in origin, rather like the aurora borealis. It's surprising that it gives off no heat, despite its brilliance.

Since I still felt weak, I held on to the Professor's arm as we explored the beach...

Uncle, isn't that the stream that led us to this cavern?

That one or another. What's the difference?

As we rounded a promontory, I saw a forest of strange trees...

What's this? Why they're...

Yes, we are in a forest of giant mushrooms!

Farther on... These lycopodiums and sigillarias are flora of the Secondary Period.

It's like a nature reserve of prehistoric plants and animals. It's incredible!

Yes, Axel, these bones are those of giant creatures, similar to the ones which walked the earth millions of years ago...

My uncle explained that we were in an area of sedimentary terrain. If ante-diluvian monsters had onced lived here, perhaps they were still around, hiding in the forests or the caves. But nothing moved in that deserted landscape...

The next morning I went for a swim in the subterranean sea.

Axel! I have calculated that...

We are eight hundred and seventy-five miles from Iceland, somewhere under Scottish Highlands. Happily, the ceiling of this cavern is solid enough. I don't think it will cave in on us!

We shall set sail first thing tomorrow.

Oh yes? Where's the ship?

to explore the shores of this underground ocean?"

"Don't fret, Axel! I've no intention of rushing into this headlong! I want to reach the far shore, where I'm certain we'll find some more tunnels. We shall set sail tomorrow!"

I automatically looked around for some means of getting to the other side.

"Right, Uncle, now explain how we're going to make this crossing without a boat!"

"There's nothing to it: we're going to build a raft!"

"But a raft is just as difficult to build as a ship and I really don't see . . ."

"Be quiet, Axel, and listen!" interrupted my uncle with an impatient gesture. "Can't you hear that hammering noise? Hans is already at work. Let's go and see how he's getting on."

After walking for a quarter of an hour, I spotted Hans hard at work and hurried to his side. Close by was a partly assembled raft made out of tree trunks, planks and beams.

"What wood is this?" I asked.

"It's fossilized wood: pine, fir, birch . . . all kinds of conifers which have been mineralized by the sea-water."

"But they are almost as hard as stone, they can't float! Coal doesn't float, after all."

"You're quite right. But although some wood changes from vegetable into mineral, other woods retain their original properties. Shall I show you?"

He picked up a piece of wood and threw it into the water. It disappeared, then bounced up again and floated.

"Are you convinced?" asked the Professor.

"Convinced that it floats, yes, but not that this land is real. Everything is so incredible!"

The next evening Hans came to tell us that the raft was ready. It was ten feet long and five feet wide and consisted of beams and trunks tied together with strong rope. The end result looked sturdy and capable of carrying us and our supplies.

O n August 13 we set to very early. We were about to sail on an untested craft across an unknown sea. The raft was pushed into the water and floated as predicted. A mast made of two staves tied together, a rug for a sail, and ropes for rigging completed our vessel. At six o'clock precisely my uncle gave the order to embark, after checking the stability of our craft. Provisions, baggage, instruments, weapons and a quantity of fresh water in canteens were lashed down on the platform. There was a light wind blowing from

19. I went back through ages...

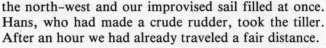

the north-west and our improvised sail filled at once. Hans, who had made a crude rudder, took the tiller. After an hour we had already traveled a fair distance.

"If this wind keeps up, we shall cover at least seventy-five miles a day. At that rate we should soon see the shore on the other side," my uncle declared.

I gave a nod of agreement and went to the front of the raft. The shores of the bay from which we had embarked were opening out, inviting us to sail onwards into this subterranean sea which stretched in its vastness before our eyes. Heavy black clouds were mirrored in the blue-green water. Soon the horizon all around us was no more than a faint line and, if it had not been for the wake of the rudder, I would have thought that we were motionless on the gloomy waters.

We had been under way for several hours when, at about midday, some giant seaweed appeared around the raft. I had heard about these plants which take root in the sea bottom and grow up to the surface, forming barriers which can impede a ship's progress. Giant seaweed once terrified Christopher Columbus' men as they crossed the Sargasso Sea. But I never dreamt that seaweed as monstrous as that on the Lidenbrock Sea could exist. We left a forest of the stuff to starboard, and I tried to guess how thick it was, knowing that we could never have sailed through it.

What natural force could have produced such plants, similar to those which invaded the oceans in the early stages of our planet's formation?

Our voyage continued monotonously the next day. There was nothing on the horizon and everything around us remained bathed in the same silvery light. Hans had secured the tiller and let the raft go with the wind. The Professor was engrossed in his figures and asked me to note down even the least important observation and to record any interesting facts in the notebook which served as our log.

So, by reading through these notes I know that on Friday August 14, at midday, Hans fastened a hook to a line, baited it with a small chunk of meat and cast it into the sea. He did not get a bite for two hours. Then there was a tug on the line. Hans pulled it in and landed a large fish.

"It's a sturgeon!" I cried. "I can tell by the scales!"

The fish had a flat, rounded head, and the front part of its body was covered with bony scales; it had no teeth and its tailless body was extended by fairly well-developed pectoral fins. After examining it carefully, my uncle announced:

Without a word, my uncle led me to a sandy cove...

Where did Hans find the wood to make that raft?

It's all fossil wood!

Didn't you notice all those dead trees lying around? There's enough to build a whole fleet! There are specimens from many species, all partially fossilized. The trunks are usable!

Hans finished the raft next day. It measured ten feet long by five feet wide.

On August 13 we climbed aboard...

Axel, I should like to give your name to this harbor.

If you don't mind, Uncle, I'd rather call it after your ward! Let it be known as Port Graüben!

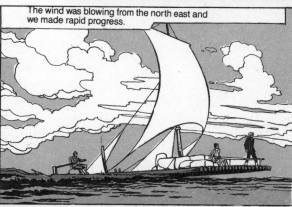

The wind was blowing from the north east and we made rapid progress.

Towards noon we passed close to a mass of giant seaweed.

Hans tied a hook to a length of rope and started to fish. Suddenly...

It's a sturgeon!

No Axel, this fish is one of an extinct species. Its fossils are sometimes found in Devonian strata. Still it does look like a sturgeon.

Hans baited his line again and lowered it into the sea. More fish took the bait. I began to daydream about this living museum of paleontology...

I dreamed I was seeing magnificent turtles as big as floating islands...

"This fish belongs to a family which has been extinct for millions of years. Its fossils have been found in sedimentary strata."

"So, we've captured one of the inhabitants of our primitive seas!"

"You can see for yourself that it bears no relation to modern species. In addition, there is one particular feature which is found in most fishes living in subterranean waters."

"What's that?"

"It's blind!"

"Blind?"

I took another look at the struggling fish and saw that my uncle was right—it had no eyes.

The line was baited again and thrown back into the sea. This area was teeming with fish for within two hours we caught some twenty specimens belonging to extinct species. None of them had eyes.

The sea was deserted, completely deserted. I looked up, but the sky was as empty as the sea.

It was so eerie that my imagination got the better of me. I thought I could see huge turtles from the Tertiary Period floating on the sea. In the air I saw voracious pterodactyls and, on the shores, I imagined those monsters which were the ancestors of our reptiles and of the first mammals.

All this apparently vanished universe lived again in my mind's eye. Following my waking dream through, I went back through the ages which, long before man walked the earth, preceded the appearance of the first living organisms.

20. The mere thought of prehistoric animals filled me with fear.

Suddenly a voice made me jump:
"What's the matter?"

Looking round, I saw my uncle standing next to me: "Axel, what's wrong? You almost fell into the sea without realizing!"

As he spoke, Hans took hold of my arm and pulled me back from the edge. If it had not been for him I would have drowned.

"I'm beginning to wonder whether this is all too much for your sanity," continued my uncle sympathetically. "Do you feel ill?"

"No, I'm fine. I was daydreaming, but it's over now. My giddiness has gone. Is everything all right?"

"Yes, there's a fair wind, and we're making good progress. But there's no sign of the far shore, not even a hint that we may be approaching it."

I shielded my eyes and looked towards the distant horizon, but there was nothing but sea, and the watery horizon merging with the clouds in the sky.

...and over this fish filled sea soared flocks of voracious pterodactyls...

On the shores, the great mammals which followed the reptiles were walking. Gigantic monsters, mastodons, mammoths, pachyderms, ancestors of the modern elephant...

Protopithecas, the first monkeys to appear on earth, were feeding on leaves, fruit and grass.

And finally, some birds with vast wingspans, bigger than ostriches, were wheeling and soaring, sometimes colliding with the roof or our immense cavern...

What's the matter, Axel? You almost fell into the sea!

Luckily, Hans had dragged me back...

How are you feeling now?

I'm all right. I was daydreaming, that's all. Don't worry...

Ahead of us the sea still merged with the sky. There was no land in sight. A week passed. Still nothing...

Are we really still on Saknussemm's trail? Can he have crossed this ocean?

My uncle decided to take some soundings.

Even at twelve hundred feet, the pickaxe was not touching the bottom. When we pulled it up, we were amazed...

How can this be? What does it mean?

CHAPTER 9

Saturday August 15. The sea seemed to go on for ever, limitless, monotonous. My uncle was pacing the length of the raft, training his binoculars first in one direction, then in another. There was obviously nothing new to be seen, for he was getting impatient and kept folding and unfolding his arms with an annoyed expression on his face.

I decided that my uncle was reverting to his temperamental old self, and that he would have been that way all along, had not my mishaps and brushes with death shaken him out of his normal attitudes. Since my recovery he had returned to his old ways. Why was he so impatient today? It was hard to understand, for we had ideal weather for our journey. The wind was favorable and the raft sped over the water.

"You seem worried, Uncle," I said, seeing him lift his binoculars to his eyes yet again.

"Worried? No!"

"Impatient, then?"

"With good reason!"

"But we are making excellent progress . . ."

"What difference does that make? This ocean carries on for ever! I thought we would have reached the other side within two days, but there's no sign of land, and we have already sailed 150 miles or more. And while we're on the water we cannot go further underground. I didn't come here for a boating trip!"

"But aren't we following the same route as Arne Saknussemm?"

"That's the trouble. I'm beginning to wonder whether he ever set eyes on this subterranean sea! Did he cross it? Perhaps that stream we followed misled us!"

● They are blind; none of them have eyes.
●● Axel was daydreaming . . .
●●● While he was on the water, he could not go further underground; he didn't come for a boating trip!

86

"As far as I'm concerned, I'm glad we came this far. The view is magnificent . . . ."

"I didn't come here to admire the view! I have set myself a task and I fully intend to see it through!"

I decided I had better keep quiet. It was obvious that my uncle was on the verge of one of his terrible fits of temper.

Sunday August 16. More of the same, except that the wind freshened. The shadow of our sail on the sea was as clearly defined as ever. At intervals the Professor tied a pickaxe to the end of a rope and let it down into the water but, even when all 1200 feet of the rope had been paid out, the pickaxe had still not touched bottom. When we hauled it in, Hans drew our attention to the tool which bore some fresh marks.

"Tänder, tänder," he repeated several times, opening and closing his mouth in an attempt at sign language.

"Teeth!" I exclaimed, looking more closely at the iron bar.

Hans nodded. Something had bitten into the metal. But what sort of creature could have done it? An amazingly strong one. Was it an enormous reptile? One of a species which had managed to survive at the bottom of that strange sea? I could not drag my eyes away from the bar and a shiver ran down my spine.

Monday August 17. I tried to remember what I had learned about these prehistoric animals which, coming after the molluscs, crustaceans and fishes, preceded the mammals on earth. These monsters were monarchs of the sea during the Jurassic period. At that stage they were true giants, and their modern descendants — crocodiles and alligators — are scaled–down versions of those mammoth beings of primitive times. The mere thought of such beasts filled me with fear. Although they had vanished from the earth long before man appeared, their fossilized bones had been miraculously preserved in limestone and sedimentary soil, and had enabled the paleontologists to reconstruct their anatomy.

Hamburg Museum had one of these skeletons. The animal to which it belonged measured thirty feet in length. Was I — an inhabitant of the earth — destined to come face to face with one of the last representatives of a vanished species? No, it was impossible! Yet the teethmarks on the iron bar were there to prove that what I feared was, in fact, a reality. I scanned the sea. It was as calm and flat as ever, but I felt a dreadful premonition. I sensed that danger was close at hand. It was like the calm before the storm.

"What on earth possessed my uncle to take those soundings?" I asked myself. "What if he disturbed a beast in his lair?"

I took a look at our guns and satisfied myself that they were loaded and in good condition. My uncle saw me do it and nodded his approval. He then pointed towards some large concentric rings of moving water which implied that something was stirring below the surface. But nothing more happened that day.

Tuesday August 18. The day passed uneventfully. Evening came, or rather the time when our drooping eyelids told us we should be asleep. It was like sailing in the latitudes of the midnight sun: the light was constant, unrelenting, tiring on our eyes. Hans was at the tiller. My uncle was asleep and I took advantage of the peace and quiet to doze a little.

21. ...a noise in the distance, like a continuous roar.

Suddenly a violent jolt brought me awake and to my feet, all in one instant. The raft was lifted up into the air with staggering force and dropped back on to the sea some hundred feet away.

Roused from his slumbers, my uncle turned to me:

"What's happened?" he asked. "Have we hit a rock?"

Hans pointed to a blackish mass about a quarter of a mile away which was leaping in and out of the water. I tried to see what it was and exclaimed:

"It's a huge dolphin!"

"So it is," agreed my uncle. "And over there is an enormous reptile which looks remarkably like a stegosaurus!"

"And farther on a colossal crocodile, you can see its huge jaws and pointed teeth. Look, it's disappearing!"

"A whale! I can see its enormous fins and the water coming up through its blowers!"

Two thick liquid columns were rising high into the sky. One blow from the tail of any of those monsters could have broken our raft in two like a straw. We clung to the mast, spellbound by this fascinating yet terrible sight. Hans was trying to steer us away, putting the tiller up but, when he turned round, he saw some other creatures, just as frightening: a turtle with a shell forty feet across and a serpent thirty feet long, darting its hideous head back and forth above the waves.

There was no escape. The two reptiles were moving around the raft in everdecreasing circles, getting closer and closer. The slightest hesitation would be fatal. I seized a rifle, but what use were bullets? They would only bounce off the scales with which the two animals

● It could be an enormous reptile.
●● A huge dolphin.

 Some creature has bitten into the iron. You can see the marks! It must be incredibly strong!

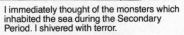  I immediately thought of the monsters which inhabited the sea during the Secondary Period. I shivered with terror.

I'm glad our guns are in good condition!

You're right! We may need them!

 Those ripples on the surface of the sea mean that something's stirring. We must keep our eyes peeled!

 As I had feared, on the night of August 18...

AAAGH!

What's happening?

 By the diffused light of this underground world, we saw the monster which had almost upturned the raft. It was terrifying!

An ichthyosaurus!

 Soon afterwards, Hans pointed to something else in the water...

It's a plesiosaurus, the enemy of the ichthyosaurus!

 Battle was joined. The two monsters attacked each other furiously, withdrew, attacked again, trying to bite each other...

 They threw up mountains of water which threatened to drown us. The two beasts were fighting with no holds barred. Hans and I stood ready to fire if the monsters came any nearer...

 After two hours the victorious ichthyosaurus raised its head out of the water. The plesiosaurus was mortally wounded.

were covered. Rigid with terror I watched them come nearer. I raised my rifle and was about to pull the trigger when Hans stopped me. The two monsters passed within a hundred yards of the raft and attacked one another. They were so set on battle that they did not even see us. A fierce fight began. Mountainous waves broke on the raft, which was tossed about so violently that we came close to capsizing. Hissing and roaring, the two beasts were locked together determined on mutual destruction. My uncle managed to contain his excitement and explained:

"You see the serpent that I thought was a stegosaurus? I recognize it now, it's a plesiosaurus. Its body is covered with an enormous shell and its neck, which is disproportionately elongated, is as supple as a snake's. The other reptile, the one which looks like a crocodile, is an ichthyosaurus."

Hans confirmed that there were indeed only two monsters before us, and that we had been confused by seeing different parts of their bodies at different times.

The struggle lasted for two hours without any sign of the savage beasts letting up in their cruelty. There were moments when, thrashing the sea with their enormous tails, they came dangerously near to us. Then, all of a sudden they disappeared, creating a giant whirlpool. Soon afterwards, the plesiosaurus' head broke the surface. The monster was writhing and twisting in ghastly convulsions. It was not long before we realized that the beast had lost part of its body and that these were its death throes. Its movements gradually became less violent until eventually the creature's inert corpse floated to the surface.

CHAPTER 10

Wednesday August 19. A brisk wind at last carried us away from the scene of the battle. Hans went back to the tiller and my uncle, briefly distracted by the fight, returned to his examination of the sea. The water became calm again and the world around us grew still.

Thursday August 20. The wind that morning was variable. It was a warm day and the raft was traveling at about nine knots. Towards noon we heard a noise in the distance. It was like a continuous roar.

"The sea must be breaking on some rock or islet in the distance," the Professor decided.

Hans hauled himself up to the top of the mast but could see nothing. The hours passed, but the noise continued, although it did not increase in volume. I suggested to my uncle that it might be the sound of rapids or an enormous waterfall. He shook his head without speaking. But, if I was wrong, where was the sound coming from?

I peered at the horizon, looked up at the clouds, but the sky was calm, the sea tranquil and unchanging. I searched through my bags, extracted an empty bottle, and threw it into the sea. If the noise came from a waterfall or a whirlpool, then the bottle would be drawn towards it. But it bobbed about in the water, staying just where I had thrown it.

At about four o'clock that afternoon Hans climbed up the mast again. He searched the arc of the horizon in front of the raft. Suddenly his eyes fixed on a certain point.

"He's seen something," said my uncle.

Hans slid down and came over to us:

"Der nere!" he said tonelessly.

"Over there?" inquired my uncle.

● The plesiosaurus, a kind of serpent.
●● As if the sea was breaking on some rock or islet in the distance.

Seizing his binoculars, he trained them in the direction which Hans had indicated. His gaze was riveted on what he saw, and he looked at it for what seemed an interminable length of time.

"He's right!" he said at last.

"What is it? What can you see?"

"A huge jet of water rising above the waves."

"Is it another whale or something like it?"

"It could be."

"Well, let's head west. I don't want to tangle with any more of those monsters!"

"We'll see," replied the Professor noncommittally.

Hans calmly returned to the tiller and held it firmly. The louder the noise grew, the more puzzled I became. What kind of beast could take in such a quantity of water and shoot it out continuously, without a pause?

At eight o'clock we were about three or four miles from what I imagined to be a giant whale. It was perfectly still and seemed to be asleep. Waves lapped its sides and the column of water rose to a height of five hundred feet before raining down on the sea with a deafening racket.

I suddenly felt terrified. I realized that we were probably sailing to our deaths and I rebelled against the obstinacy of my uncle, who was blindly courting danger and defying fate.

22. The ball turned red, burst and scattered like raindrops.

All at once Hans stood up and, pointing towards the black mass for which we were heading, cried: "Holme!"

"An island!" my uncle translated.

"An island?" I said sceptically.

"Yes, Hans is right!" the Professor insisted, roaring with laughter. "I should have thought of it before!"

"But what's that column of water?"

"It's a geyser, that's all! You can find them by the thousand in Iceland."

And, as we drew closer, I could see that I had been mistaken. The island looked very like a vast whale, with a little hill of lava for a head. The geyser was breathtaking. The enormous jet, projected upwards by volcanic forces, spat its vaporous stream up as far as the lowest cloud layer. There were no patches of escaping steam or hot springs around it. All the escaping energy was concentrated in that one geyser.

"Let's land!" said the Professor.

But we had to avoid the waterspout which would have sunk the raft in an instant. Hans steered us to the other end of the island. I jumped ashore, while our guide stayed at his post, ready for anything that might happen.

My uncle and I were walking on a huge rock of granite mixed with a siliceous tufa. The ground was burning hot beneath our feet. When we had gone a few yards we caught sight of a wide basin from which the geyser was spouting. Plunging a thermometer into the boiling water I found that the mercury shot up and registered 163°C.

So, this water must have been heated up in the bowels of the earth and the precious theory expounded by my dear uncle, Professor Lidenbrock, was proved false. I took malicious delight in pointing this out to him.

"What of it?" he replied curtly. "That doesn't prove me wrong!"

Knowing that whatever I said I would come up against his usual stubbornness and be silenced by some arbitrary and probably false counterarguments, I decided to change the subject.

Apart from the geyser, there was nothing of interest on the island, and we soon returned to the raft. Hans had been busy checking our supplies and adjusting the ropes. When I was once more aboard, I made some calculations and, comparing these figures with those in my notebook, found that we had sailed 1,300 miles from our point of embarkation.

Friday August 21. By morning the giant geyser had disappeared below the horizon. The wind had freshened and was taking us along rapidly. I had a feeling that the weather — if one can use that word when talking of such an environment — was about to change. Vapor rose from the sea, the clouds were lower and greenish in color, and the air was charged with electricity. In short, if I had been on the surface of the earth, I would have said that a storm was in the offing. At about ten o'clock, the signs became clearer. Violent gusts of wind alternating with periods of deathly calm ruffled the sea.

The Professor, to whom I revealed my concern, did not deign to reply. He was in a filthy temper and I could easily guess the reason: he had had enough of sailing on this endless sea.

"We're going to have a storm!" I announced, in an attempt to break the tension. "It might be a good idea to reef the sail and take down the mast. A sudden gust might snap it in two!"

"No, no, a thousand times no!" raged my uncle. "Let the wind blow us towards islands, rocks, solid land, even if the raft is smashed in the process!"

He had hardly finished his sentence when a distinct change occurred on the horizon. The vapor-laden clouds were transformed into water, and the air,

Aha! The ichthyosaurus has disappeared. Perhaps he's gone back to his under-water lair.

...or else he's coming back!

Fortunately, the wind freshened and took us away from the battle-ground. We saw no further sign of the monsters. But, on August 20...

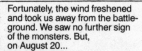
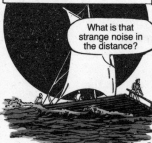

What is that strange noise in the distance?

Hans pointed to the south...

Der nere!

That must mean "over there". Heavens! A towering column of water!

If it's a creature like the ones we met earlier, we should steer well clear of it! To judge by the volume of water it's spouting, that beast must be colossal!

We haven't come all this way to be prudent. We're going to take a look!

Towards eight o'clock that evening we were within a few miles of the monster. Hans said calmly...

An island!

An island! It was true: Hans was right. The water was a magnificent geyser, like ones we had seen in Iceland.

We shall name this island after you, Axel!

Thank you, Uncle! Phew! What a relief! It isn't a monster after all!

The next day we turned away from the island. I worked out our position and found that we were under England, one thousand three hundred miles from Iceland.

Hmm! There's a storm brewing!

Suddenly the sky grew dark and the hurricane struck...

The sail! We must reef it in!

No! We must let the wind take us, otherwise we'll never cross this accursed sea!

The storm raged for several days. On August 24, the raft was still drifting, a plaything of the wind and the sea, and we saw some extraordinary sights...

And uncle still insists we keep the sail up!

sucked violently into the vacuum, blew with hurricane intensity. Rain pelted down on us, the sea went wild, waves rose up around us. The raft was lifted up, tilted and fell forward. My uncle slipped and tumbled to the deck. I dragged myself across to him to help him up. I found him clutching a piece of rope attached to the mast. Hans still held the tiller and was watching the sail which looked ready to split. I shouted:

"The sail! We must lower it!"

"No!" my uncle replied.

"Nej," added Hans, shaking his head.

The rain was coming down in torrents, the sea boiled and the sky was a mass of electrical activity. Flashes of lightning mingled with rolls of thunder. The hail bounced off our tools and our weapons like gunshots. The metal parts crackled from the thunderbolts. It seemed as though the heavenly fire was picking out our unfortunate raft.

I was in a daze, deafened by the unholy racket. Instinctively I hung on to the mast, which bent as though it would break before the violence of the tempest!

(At this point my notes became very sketchy. They were limited to a few brief, unconnected jottings. Despite their shortcomings, they still provide a faithful portrayal of my feelings and of the conditions in which they were written.)

Sunday August 23. The night was terrible, and by Sunday morning the storm showed no sign of abating. We were trapped in a world of perpetual noise and movement, unable to hear ourselves speak. The lightning flashed continuously, the rain beat down twice as hard and the din was so great that, if a powder magazine had blown up right next to us, we would not have noticed. The thunder gave us no peace: it was as though the clouds were bent on self-destruction.

All day our raft was tossed about like a nutshell, half submerged, pounded by the waves. We would have been swept off it long ago if we hadn't taken the precaution of tying ourselves down.

What would become of us? My uncle lay flat on the raft, holding on like grim death to the baggage. It began to feel hotter, so I decided to look at the thermometer. It read . . . (the figure is illegible).

Monday August 24. Would this tempest never end? Was there any reason why this atmosphere, much denser than that on the surface and saturated with electricity, should change? I felt shattered, my bones ached with tiredness and strain. Hans was soaked to

● An enormous jet of vaporous steam projected upwards by volcanic forces.
●● They sailed 1,300 miles from the point of embarkation on the Lidenbrock Sea.
●●● They had taken the precaution of tying themselves down with ropes.

the skin, as were we all, but he remained as silent as ever. The raft was now being driven south–east by the gusting wind, and we had traveled about 100 miles from the island with the geyser. At noon, the storm blew even stronger. The waves curled over our heads before breaking behind us. We hadn't been able to talk for three days. We opened our mouths, moved our lips, but no one understood a word. My uncle managed to struggle over to me and tried to make himself heard. I attempted to read his lips, and I think he said: "We are done for."

I made signs to him that we should lower the sail. This time he caught my meaning and nodded. At that very moment, a ball of fire appeared. The mast and sail were spirited away. There was a deafening clap of thunder. The fireball was moving slowly, spinning like a top, coming nearer, moving away, going up, then down. Rigid with terror we watched it touch the powder box. Would the ammunition explode? I waited with bated breath for the box to catch fire and blow up the raft and its passengers . . . The dazzling ball moved on. It headed towards Hans, who stared fixedly at it, then towards the Professor who flung himself flat to get out of its way, and finally towards me. Paralyzed with fear, I prepared to face death. There was a smell of nitrous gas. It seared my throat and lungs. I felt I would suffocate . . . .

I could not move my foot: it was as if it were riveted to the raft. Eventually I understood what had happened. The electrical fireball had magnetized all the metal objects on board, and the nails in my boot were clinging to an iron plate let into the planks.

At last, with a supreme effort of strength and will, I snatched my foot away just as the fireball was about to touch it . . . .

Suddenly we were treated to a firework display. The ball turned red, burst and scattered fire like raindrops.

The phenomenon only lasted a few seconds, then everything went dark. But I had time to see my uncle, squatting at the foot of what was the mast, and Hans, still holding the tiller . . .

23. 'Fate is playing tricks on us!'

Tuesday August 25. I don't know how long I was unconscious. When I came round the storm was still at its height, with flashes of lightning mingling with thunderclaps.

Then I thought I heard a new and different sound . . . the crash of waves breaking on rocks! . . .

Here ends what I called my "log", which somehow survived the storm.

The collision of our raft with the rocks happened so suddenly that I can remember nothing of it. The first thing I recall seeing is a hot sandy beach where I awoke to find my uncle by my side. Hans, our faithful guide, went back to the rocks against which our raft had been dashed, to see what he could salvage of our belongings.

The rain was still pelting down, but with that extra ferocity which announces the end of a storm. We took shelter beneath some overhanging rocks which enabled us to light a fire and cook some food. Then, exhausted by three days and nights of harrowing struggles and no sleep, we lay down and were soon lost to the world.

We awoke to a beautiful day. The sea and the sky were perfectly calm. There was no trace of the storm. The Professor seemed in a good mood, as he proved by asking me cheerfully:

"Well, Axel? Had a good night's rest, eh?"

"Very good, Uncle, but I still feel stiff."

"Oh, a bit of exercise will soon put that right!"

"You seem in fine fettle this morning! Any particular reason?"

"We've arrived, my boy!"

"Where? At the end of the expedition?"

"No, at the end of that tedious voyage! Now we can turn our backs on the sea and continue our downward progress."

"Have you thought about how we're to get back?"

"Get back? Wait until we've reached our destination!"

"But, Uncle, I would like to know how we're going to return to the surface!"

"That's simple enough. Once we've reached the center of the earth, we shall find another way up, or we'll go back the same way we came. There's no reason why we shouldn't!"

"If we opt for the latter course, we'll have to rebuild the raft."

"Naturally!"

"Have you thought about provisions? Will there be enough?"

"Well, I think so. Hans rescued the bulk of the cargo. He's down on the beach. Let's go and find out."

The Icelander was surrounded by piles of objects which he was in the midst of sorting. Our loyal friend had fished out most of our equipment and supplies while we were sleeping. All that was missing were our guns, but, thanks to its watertight box, our supply of powder was perfectly dry.

"Where are the instruments?" I asked.

Suddenly, we were confronted by a strange and terrifying thing...

What's that? It's a fireball!

It comes from the upper levels of this subterranean world. It must be some kind of electrical phenomenon.

The burning ball ripped away both the mast and the sail...

Then it headed back towards us, liable to burn us to a cinder at any moment...

We're done for!

Suddenly the fireball disintegrated right over our heads. I passed out...

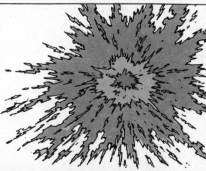

When I came to, the next day, the wind was driving us along...

What's that noise? It sounds like waves breaking on rocks!

We made several wild guesses. Suddenly we hit some underground rocks...

AAAGH!

I owed my life to Hans. It was thanks to him that I was neither drowned nor crushed to death. He laid me down on the sand...

The next day brought glorious weather.

At last we've crossed that interminable sea. From now on we shall travel by land and look for a way down into the center of the earth.

I admire his courage! Nothing gets him down!

Hans had managed to salvage the instruments and supplies. My uncle thanked him warmly.

We have enough provisions to last us four months. There's plenty to keep us going until we reach the surface and I'll give a banquet for my colleagues at the Academy with the leftovers!

The manometer is the most precious of all the instruments; with it we can work out our depth and know when we've reached the center of the earth. Without it, we might well have carried on until we reached the Antipodes! Let's see what the compass says!

"The most vital one, the manometer, is intact," replied the Professor. "I need it for calculating our depth so that we know when we are at the center."

"And the compass?"

"There it is! And here are the thermometer and the chronometer! How would we manage without Hans! . . ."

We had food for another four months. My uncle was well satisfied and suggested:

"Let's work out our position. That storm made me lose my bearings. All the same, I should not be surprised to find that we're somewhere beneath the Mediterranean!"

"That sounds unlikely!"

"Unlikely, perhaps. Impossible, no! But it doesn't really matter whether we're under Turkey or the Atlantic, come to that, as long as we keep the direction constant. We need the compass to make sure of that!"

The Professor walked over to the rock on which Hans had laid out the instruments, picked up the compass, placed it horizontally and watched the needle which swung from side to side for a few moments, then settled.

My uncle rubbed his eyes, looked again, then turned to me disbelievingly.

"What's the matter?" I asked.

He motioned me to go and look for myself. The north to which it was pointing was what we had presumed to be the south! Instead of pointing towards the sea, it was directed towards the beach behind us!

I shook the compass and tried again. The needle took up the same position as before.

There was no disputing the conclusion. The wind must have changed during the storm, blowing the raft back to the shore from which we had started!

● It turned red and burst; it looked like fireworks or like raindrops of fire.
●● The expedition towards the center of the earth could continue.
●●● For four months. Their food would last that long.

CHAPTER 11

It would be impossible to describe Professor Lidenbrock's emotions when he made this unpleasant discovery. First came amazement, then disbelief, and finally anger, perfectly justifiable anger at that. That tiring, dangerous voyage had all been for nothing! We had to start all over again! Instead of going forward, we had been going back!

However, my uncle soon calmed down.

"Fate is playing tricks on us," he said. "I could even say that the elements are in league to prevent us finding the way. But, upon my word, I shall not give in! We'll see who is the victor, man or nature!"

The Professor was standing on a rock, shaking his fist at the whole world. I considered it advisable to intervene and try to pacify him. He allowed me to put to him, without interruption, what I saw as the obvious and irrefutable arguments for going back up to the surface. First, we had a limited supply of food; second, the raft, which had been battered by the storm, was incapable of withstanding a long voyage.

When I had finished listing the numerous problems with which we would have to contend, my uncle announced, in a tone which brooked no disagreement:

"We shall leave tomorrow! Since fate has brought us here, I intend to explore this part of the coast."

You will understand this remark more readily when I tell you that we had fetched up on the northern shore, but farther east than our original point of departure. That being the case, our obvious course was to explore our surroundings.

24. I applauded his imaginary lecture enthusiastically.

Leaving Hans to repair the raft, we set off. We were walking on sedimentary soil, littered with the shells and bones of vanished species. My uncle peered between the rocks, looking for a tunnel. We had walked about a mile along the shore when we noticed a change in the landscape. The ground seemed to have been convulsed by upheavals of the strata beneath, due to some intense volcanic activity which had dislocated the earth's crust. It was hard going over these accumulations of rocks — granite mixed with flint, quartz and alluvial deposits — but at the other side we found a vast plain covered with bleached skeletons. It looked like an immense cemetery where thousands of animals had died. The mounds of bones, relics of the different stages in animal evolution, were amazing. Filled with curiosity we moved forward, crushing underfoot the fossil remains of prehistoric animals. When he first saw this staggering sight, my uncle lifted his arms to the sky. His gaping mouth, his head turning from side to side, everything about him indicated that he was utterly stupefied.

But even greater wonders awaited us.

The Professor suddenly stopped short, bent down and picked up a yellowed skull. Trembling with excitement he shouted:

"Axel! Axel! A human skull!"

Equally astonished, I replied:

"A human skull? But that's impossible!"

"But I tell you, Axel, this is the skull of a man!"

After a brief silence Professor Lidenbrock, carried away by his temperament, assumed his role of university lecturer. Forgetting where we were, he seemed to think that he was back at Hamburg University, in front of his pupils. Addressing an imaginary audience, he began in a scholarly tone:

"Gentlemen, I have the honor of introducing you to a man of the Quartenary Period. Eminent scholars have denied his existence, while others have affirmed it. If those who are sceptical could be here with us today, they would soon see the error of their ways. This man was indisputably a Caucasian. Yes, he belonged to our own, white race. No, Gentlemen, do not laugh! This is a man who knew the monsters and mastodons whose bones lie preserved in this amphitheatre. The authenticity of this fossil cannot be doubted."

I applauded his lecture enthusiastically.

This was not the only skull. With every step we found more. To tell the truth, the sight of the remains of generations of men and animals, lying intermingled in this vast cemetery, was deeply disturbing. Their existence gave rise to a question to which neither my uncle nor myself knew the answer. What catastrophe had caused their deaths? Had they lived here, in this subterranean world, beneath this pretence of a sky?

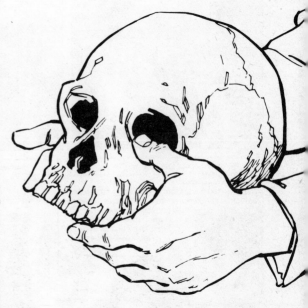

● The limited supply of food and the raft, which had been battered by the storm.
●● The Professor and Axel found the skull of a man.

We were in for a shock...

It's not possible, Axel!

Oh! The magnetized needle is showing north when we thought it would say south. That means...

Yes! The wind must have changed back during the storm. It's brought us back to where we started. So we can't be very far from the place where we embarked!

Fate and the elements are in league against me! But I shall show them that I am stronger than they are. I refuse to give in, to go back or to retreat. We'll see who is the victor, man or nature!

Since we're here, we might as well take a look round, Axel!

As we walked...

What creatures wore these shells?

Glyptodons, enormous chelonians, distant ancestors of our turtles...

We talked about this sea, and its strange properties...

This sea must have formed gradually from water which seeped through the earth's crust. Internal heat causes evaporation which produces those clouds. The electrical phenomena we witnessed have no other origin.

Your reasoning is sound, Axel. However incredible nature's works may seem, there is always a reasonable explanation.

Suddenly we came upon a vast plain covered with skeletons...

Amazing!

Bones as far as the eye can see!

It's the most extraordinary collection of prehistoric animal fossils that one could possibly imagine! They belong to the whole range of species and there are thousands of them!

Soon the professor's surprise changed to stupefaction...

Axel! Come and see!

A human skull!

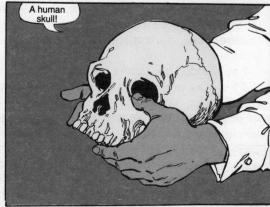

Until now, the only living beings we had encountered had been fish and reptiles. Were we to believe that the human race still existed in the bowels of the earth?

For more than an hour we wandered through this wilderness of skeletons. What else would we discover? What surprises lay in store? I imagined all kinds of things. We had long since left the sea–shore. I was following my uncle, who was heading deeper into the interior, too absorbed to single out landmarks which could guide us on our return journey. For some inexplicable reason, the light shone uniformly on everything, illuminating objects on all their sides, so that there were no shadows. You might have thought yourself on the equator at midday, with the sun directly above. In this peculiar atmosphere the mountains, rocks, and bones around us looked stark and flat.

25. Some moving silhouettes...?

After walking a mile or so, we reached the edge of a forest. It consisted of trees which resembled those of the Tertiary Period on earth. There were palm trees, belonging to extinct species, pines, yews, cypresses — all linked together by a network of creepers. The ground was covered with a thick blanket of moss and bracken. Strangely, all the trees, shrubs and plants were of the same brownish hue.

My uncle plunged without breaking his stride into this giant thicket. I followed him with some misgivings. My feelings were that, if nature had created this impressive source of vegetable food, we would probably meet some fearsome animals. In the vast clearings there was a mass of leguminous plants, shrubs, eucalyptus trees, oaks, Lapland birches, Norwegian firs. It was a display which would have made a biologist's mouth water!

I suddenly stopped dead. Putting out a hand, I held my uncle back. Although it was very dark in this forest, with its riot of trees and shrubs, there was enough light for us to make out the shapes of things. I thought I had seen some vague outlines, some moving silhouettes . . . .

Carried away by his discovery, my uncle began to lecture an imaginary audience...

Gentlemen, I have the honor of introducing you to a man from the Quarternary Period. Great scientists have denied his existence, others have affirmed it. If they were here today they would be forced to bow to the evidence. The skeptics would be silenced!

This skull is that of a member of the Caucasian race. That is the white race, our own! Please, Gentlemen, do not laugh!

Unless this man came here as I did, as a tourist or a scientific pioneer, the authenticity of this evidence is beyond question!

Bravo, uncle!

How astonishing it is to see these generations of men and animals lying together in this necropolis! Did their bones get collected here by some earthquake, or did they choose this immense cemetery as their deathbed?

The only living things we have seen are fish or reptiles. But this subterranean world may well be the home of mammals or a race of primitive men!

We had long left the seashore which was at the other side of this skeleton-covered plain.

Axel, have you noticed that the light shining down on us has no visible source and that there are no shadows? It's as though we were on the Equator at noon, when the sun is at its zenith. Everything looks one-dimensional: rocks, mountains...

We are like that man in the **Tales of Hoffman** who lost his shadow...

After walking for about a mile we came to the edge of a magnificent dense forest, consisting of trees and plants from the Tertiary Period.

My uncle plunged into it without hesitation. Since nature had given birth to such luxurious vegetation, why shouldn't this forest shelter the mammals which lived during the Tertiary Period?

CHAPTER 12

I blinked hard then looked again, in case I had imagined them. No! Those were definitely the shapes of mastodons, similar to the ones whose remains were discovered, virtually intact, in the marshes of Ohio! I could hear the sound of saplings being brushed aside, of foliage being ripped off trees, of monsters devouring their vegetative prey.

My dream about all these monsters from the Tertiary and Quartenary Periods was coming true. There we were, my uncle and I, far below the surface of the earth, the only witnesses to this prehistoric drama!

The Professor was standing awestruck, his eyes glued to the spectacle. He seized my arm and hissed:

"Come along! Forward!"

"No!" I cried. "It would be madness! Why disturb them? Why provoke those monsters? Let's go while we can! No man could hope to brave the anger of those beasts without taking the consequences!"

"But you're wrong, Axel! Look over there! Is that or is that not a man? Or am I imagining him?"

I shrugged my shoulders and looked where he pointed. I was forced to accept the evidence of my eyes. Less than a quarter of a mile away, leaning against the trunk of a giant eucalyptus tree, I saw a human being who was apparently looking after the grazing herd of mastodons.

He was nothing like the fossil creature whose skull we had found in the cemetery and who would have been about six feet tall. This man was a giant, at least twelve feet tall, with an abundance of facial hair. In his hand was a stout branch, which he was probably using as a shepherd uses his crook.

We stood there dumbstruck. At any moment we might catch that strange creature's attention and, since

● The trees resembled those of the Tertiary Period on earth.
●● It was apparently looking after the grazing herd of mastodons.
●●● The dagger blade was of pure steel.

105

we had no guns, we would be defenceless. I felt that discretion was the greater part of valor and led my uncle, for once unprotesting, away from the scene.

When I recall the episode, now that I am quite calm again, I wonder whether we were victims of our imagination. Is it possible that I really did see a human being in that unreal subterranean world? I prefer to believe that it was some kind of ape: a protopitheca or mesopitheca like the ones whose fossils are found in sedimentary soil, and which were very much taller than modern man.

Meanwhile, we had left the forest and were hurrying instinctively towards the shore. In our panic-stricken state, incapable of rational thought, the sea drew us like a magnet. When we reached it we made a depressing discovery. Looking at the compass, I deduced that we were close to the point from which we had set sail, and I could even recognize certain features of the landscape — the shape of a rock, the sweep of a bay.

I shared my thoughts with my uncle. He too seemed uncertain.

"The storm must have brought us back farther down the coast," I said. "If we follow the shoreline we're certain to come upon the cave which served as our doorway into this subterranean land."

"If that's the case," replied the Professor, "there's no point in going any further. We'd do better to return to Hans. But are you sure about this, Axel?"

"I can't be positive, because there's nothing definite to go by. All these rocks look the same. But I think that's the promontory where Hans built the raft . . ."

"We should at least be able to see our tracks," observed my uncle, "but there's no sign . . ."

26. The alchemist's signature and his very knife: what a discovery!

" I can see something!" I cried, pouncing on an object which was shining on the sand.

"What is it?"

"A dagger?"

"Does it belong to Hans?"

I looked at the knife carefully.

"No, I've never seen him with one like this."

"Well, it doesn't date from the Stone Age or the Bronze Age. This blade is pure steel . . ."

"What does that prove, Uncle?"

"That it's a sixteenth-century weapon, similar to those worn by gentlemen and big-game hunters. They used them to finish off their victims. This one is Spanish. The thickness of the rust on it shows that it's very old."

"But it can't have got here on its own!"

Suddenly...

I want to get closer.

No, Uncle! Heaven knows what would happen if those mastodons caught sight of us!

Axel! Axel! Look over there, can you see that man?

We decided we would be safer if the giant didn't see us!

It can't be! It was an ape, not a man! A protopithec! It's not possible that a human being could have survived underground! It cannot be true!

I see that you would rather accept the existence of an animal which happens to resemble a human being, a primitive ape, in fact, but how do you explain its immense size?

Yes, I would rather...

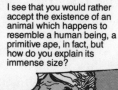

When we returned to the shore...

Look, Uncle!

A 16th-century dagger!

Someone had been there before us! My uncle was already scouring the rocks around us. Suddenly...

It's the entrance to a tunnel!

We found something even more remarkable on a granite rock...

Look Axel! Someone used the dagger to engrave these letters. They're Arne Saknussemm's initials! We're back on his trail!

It was obvious that Arne Saknussemm had come this way! I had no choice but to believe his story now...

What a strange quirk of fate! We sailed south and traveled north and came to this very spot!

Let's go and find Hans! We'll sail the raft round to this promontory which I shall name Saknussemm Point.

26/

"No, someone has been here before us. We'll soon find out his name, for I'm sure he would have marked the route to the center of the earth. Let's look!"

We skirted the cliff, moving forward slowly, all our senses alert, peering into any crack which might give access to a tunnel. When we came to the point where the sea lapped the foot of the cliff, we caught a glimpse of the entrance to a dark tunnel. There, on the granite surface, were two letters, the perfectly legible initials of that long-ago traveler.

A͢S

"Arne Saknussemm!" exclaimed the Professor. "We've caught up with him again!"

I had witnessed so many surprising and fantastic events since the beginning of our expedition that I thought I would never be astonished again. But the sight of those two letters, engraved some three hundred years earlier, left me speechless. Not only was I looking at the famous alchemist's signature, but I was also holding the very knife he had used to write it! At last I was convinced. I could no longer doubt the truth of the message I had deciphered. While I was considering these facts, Professor Lidenbrock was launching himself into one of those lyric passages for which he has such a gift.

"Marvelous genius! It is thanks to you that your fellow scientists can follow in your footsteps; travel, with no risk of going astray, those dark, subterranean tunnels. Your initials are our signposts! I too will sign my name to this wondrous adventure to which you passed me the key and the secret."

My uncle's enthusiasm was infectious and I instantly felt more cheerful. I forgot everything: the dangers of the journey, the storm, the fantastic creatures. Filled with the need for action, I told myself that I was quite capable of doing what others had done before me.

I was already moving towards the tunnel entrance when the Professor stopped me:

"Hold on! We must find Hans first and see if he has finished repairing the raft. We'll discuss it later!"

Reluctantly I followed him.

Our guide had everything ready and was waiting for us near to the raft, which was bobbing gently a few yards from the beach. We embarked silently and Hans took the tiller, steering the raft towards the promontory where we had found the inscription. We were sailing parallel to the shore in shallow water, and several times we had to move farther out to avoid

● As are the initials of Arne Saknussemm.
●● Axel and the Professor prepared the fuse. In the meantime Hans started to hollow out a hole.

partly submerged rocks. It must have been about six o'clock in the evening when we came to a gently shelving beach where we could land. I jumped on to the sand, followed by my uncle. The short trip had in no way dampened my enthusiasm.

"Come on, Uncle, let's get going! We've wasted enough time as it is!"

"All in good time, Axel, but I want to take a look at this new tunnel first."

The opening was about six feet across and was roughly circular. White–hot molten rock must have bored its way through the cliff, and the walls of the tunnel were as smooth as glass. The gallery led horizontally into the rock. We had only taken a few steps along its length when we found our way barred by a huge block. The fact that there seemed no way past it made me cry out with frustration. I looked frantically for some weak point, a crack or any way through or over it, but the rock was solid, smooth and impassable. I squatted on the ground and peered underneath. My uncle, meanwhile, was pacing up and down impatiently and exclaimed:

"I refuse to believe that Arne Saknussemm would have let himself be beaten by a lump of rock. There must be a way round and it's up to us to find it!"

"In my opinion this rock blocked the tunnel long after the scientist passed through. Look around you! Isn't it obvious that this gallery was formed by lava?"

"Whatever the case," replied the Professor, "it's in our way, so we'll hack through it with our pickaxes!"

"But it's made of granite!"

"So we'll use powder! We'll mine the obstacle and blow it up!"

"Powder!"

"Of course! Now, to work!"

Hans returned to the raft, came back with a pickaxe and started to hollow out a hole. It was very hard work, and it took him several hours of constant toil. Leaving our guide to it, I helped my uncle to prepare a fuse out of damp gunpowder wrapped in a cloth tube.

At midnight we placed the charge in the hollow, and rolled the fuse out along the floor of the gallery. All that remained was to light it!

"We'll do that tomorrow," said my uncle. "We must rest first. Goodnight!"

I reluctantly resigned myself to waiting. My sleep was full of nightmares.

Some monstrous animals were fighting, clawing and biting each other. Giant men appeared, armed with stone axes, and began to cut up an enormous whale

27. 'Five minutes to go... four... three... two... one...'

The three of us took our places on the raft and Hans steered it to the promontory.

As we entered the tunnel I felt cheerful and optimistic once more.

...but around a corner...

There's a rock blocking the tunnel!

How on earth did Saknussemm get past it?

I think the tunnel must have been blocked as a result of an earthquake long after Saknussemm passed through. We must find an opening!

No Axel! You'll never do it with a pickax. We must blast it!

It was exhausting work, but eventually a large quantity of gunpowder was placed in a hollow hacked out with pickaxes, and connected to a fuse which led out of the tunnel.

We'll light the fuse in the morning.

I had a terrible nightmare: I was surrounded by strange creatures

...and prehistoric monsters which were about to attack my uncle and myself...

We took flight and found shelter in an enormous cave

...but we were trapped inside, for reptiles, mammoths and other giant beasts were guarding the entrance. What a terrible night!

which had been washed up on the shore.

At six o'clock the next morning I was chafing at the bit. I asked my uncle whether I could be the one to light the fuse. Afterwards I would join my companions on the raft, which was still laden with our belongings. Then we would move a little way out to sea, as the explosion might well cause some of the cliff face to break away and fall into the sea, producing a miniature tidal wave.

We estimated that our fuse would burn for ten minutes, so that there would be plenty of time for us to retreat to a safe position. After a hasty breakfast, Hans and my uncle boarded the raft, while I remained ashore, holding a lighted lantern in my hand.

"Off you go," said the Professor, "and hurry!"

I made my way towards the tunnel entrance, opened the lantern and picked up the end of the fuse. My uncle looked at his chronometer, then shouted: "Now, my boy! Light it!"

I did as asked and the fuse began to crackle. I ran back to the water's edge.

"Jump aboard quickly, and let's get clear!" he shouted, as Hans pushed us off with a pole. I held my breath and the Professor's eyes were glued to his chronometer. He counted aloud:

"Five minutes to go . . . four . . . three . . . two . . . one . . ."

28. 'We're going up!' The temperature went up too...

What happened then? I suddenly had the impression that everything around us was teetering. The rockface opened and there was a gaping hole where the gallery entrance had once been. The sea rose up in fury and was soon one immense whirlpool, with our raft spinning around inside it like a blade of grass. All of a sudden the raft tipped up on end and I clung grimly to the tree–trunks from which it was made. At first I thought we were sinking. I tried to cry out, to call to my uncle, but the water was roaring so loudly that he could not hear me. Despite the darkness and the terror which was paralyzing my limbs, I realized what had happened. The rock we had blown up was not blocking up a tunnel but an abyss, and the explosion had set off a powerful earthquake. A chasm had opened up and the sea was pouring into the gulf, dragging us with it.

Deafened and bewildered we clung to the ropes, and to each other for comfort. The raft kept crashing into the walls and was liable to break up at any moment. But our collisions seemed to become less frequent and I decided that the tunnel along which we were hurtling at breakneck speed was widening. We rushed on for

The next day was August 27, a day I shall never forget. I lit the fuse...

then...

Four minutes, three, two, one! Here it comes...

BRAAUUM!

What's happening?

Something's sucking us in!

There was an immense hole where once the rocks had been. The sea water was pouring in, taking us with it...

From the darkness all around us and the deafening noise, I realized what had happened...

There must have been an enormous cavity behind the rock we blasted... The explosion produced an earthquake and the sea is emptying! This time there's no escape! We're done for!

Our dizzying fall continued. We were indeed following in Saknussemm's wake, but what a way to do it! Luckily the raft was still intact. It had not yet struck any obstacle. But what a drenching.

Luckily the deluge soon stopped. Then...

It's as I thought. We are in some shaft or other. Now the sea has reached the bottom; it will rise until it finds its own level. It will take us up like a lift.

But what if there's no way out of this shaft? If it's closed at the top the air will be compressed by the rising water and we'll be crushed!

one hour, two, maybe more.

In a quieter moment Hans managed to light a lantern and its flickering light revealed the true extent of the catastrophe. Nearly all our food had vanished and the mast had been ripped off. All that remained of our instruments were the compass and the chronometer. Our stock of ladders and ropes was reduced to a piece of cord wrapped round the planks of the raft. Through some quirk of my imagination, I forgot our immediate danger and dwelt instead on the threat posed by our dwindling supplies. Unless some miracle occurred we would die of starvation! I did not want to add to my companions' worries, so I kept this bad news to myself for the time being. Soon the lantern light began to weaken, for the wick was almost burnt out, and then we were in complete darkness once again. Our angle of descent became even sharper: we were no longer sliding over the surface of the water, but falling almost vertically. Desperately clinging to each other, we waited for the terrible nightmare to end. I cannot tell how long this continued, but suddenly I felt a shock. The craft jolted to a standstill and a spout of water fell down on us. Struggling for breath, I believed that my last hour had come . . . .

I came round a few minutes later. The drenching was over and I was gulping fresh air. Opening my eyes I saw my companions bending over me. As soon as I became fully aware of my surroundings I was struck by the silence in the gallery after the deafening din which had been assaulting my ears for hours. My uncle's words came to me like a murmur:

"We're going up!"

"What are you saying?"

"We're going up, Axel!"

I stretched out an arm and touched the wall; it grazed my hand. We were, indeed, going up — as quickly as in a lift.

"The torch, Hans!"

With great difficulty our guide managed to light it.

"Just as I thought," said my uncle. "We're in a sort of shaft. The water has reached the bottom of the abyss and is now finding its own level, carrying us up with it."

"But where to?"

"I don't know! Anything could happen . . . Let's hope that there's a way out of this shaft farther up! If it's a dead end and the air is compressed as the water rises, we shall be crushed."

"What can we do?"

"Nothing . . . except wait and say our prayers!"

We were still rising rapidly, so rapidly that we sometimes had difficulty in breathing. At the same

● It produced a powerful earthquake.
●● Hans lightened a torch.

time the temperature was increasing alarmingly. I guessed that it was about 40°C.

When I mentioned it to my uncle, he said:

"So far the facts have proved Davy's theories correct. I wonder whether we are going to reach a level where the internal heat is great enough to liquefy the rocks? If we do, we shall be burned alive!"

As we went up, the temperature went up too. We were dripping with sweat. The atmosphere was similar to that near a foundry furnace when the molten metal is being transferred into molds. We soon had to take off most of our clothes, for it felt as though they were burning our skins.

"Where are we heading for?" I shouted. "The heat source is somewhere near here and we're going straight towards it!"

"No, no!" my uncle replied. "That's impossible!"

I dipped my fingers in the water and withdrew them instantly, panic-stricken.

"The water's boiling!" I yelled.

Terror got the better of me. I was sure we were going to our deaths, but then an idea, vague at first, slowly took form in my mind. However much I tried to push it away, it came back, gnawing at my emotions. I did not dare put it into words. Meanwhile I could hear cracking noises and distant explosions. I thought I saw the walls shake.

I looked at the compass. It had gone mad! The needle was swinging from one pole to the other, with frantic jerks, under the influence of electric phenomena whose meaning was too terrible to contemplate. Was the earth's crust about to split?

29. A last surprise awaited us.

I could not stop myself shouting to my uncle:

"Look! The walls are moving! Rocks are falling all around us! There's steam coming out of the cracks and the needle's gone haywire! All the signs of an earthquake!"

"An earthquake?"

"Yes!"

"I think you're mistaken, my boy!"

"But those are the symptoms!"

"They're the symptoms of an eruption, not an earthquake."

"An eruption? Are we in the shaft of an active volcano?"

"I think so! And it's the best thing that could happen to us!"

I decided that my uncle must have gone out of his mind.

"What?" I screamed. "We're trapped in an eruption and that makes you happy? We're probably going to be burned to a crisp and thrown out by this volcano in a shower of ash and lava and you say that it's the best thing that could happen!"

The Professor looked at me over the top of his spectacles and replied deliberately:

"Yes, because it's the only way we'll reach the surface of the earth!"

A thousand ideas crossed my mind. On reflection my uncle was right, and I had never seen him so sure of himself. It was obvious that, in his eyes, we were bound to emerge unscathed from our adventure. But equally obvious was the hopelessness of our position! We were still rising, carried up by the volcanic forces. The water beneath our raft was boiling, and there were molten lava and rocks lower down. We were in the chimney of a very active volcano — of that there was no doubt!

Were we underneath Iceland? Would we come out through Hecla or one of the lesser-known volcanoes? The hours passed with painful slowness. We seemed to be going up even faster. Some colossal force, generated by the fires in the earth's core, was pushing us upwards at an unimaginable speed. To my horror I saw the vertical walls rushing by, with occasional flashes of lurid light and huge tunnels from which clouds of toxic gases and tongues of flame leaped out at us.

"Look, Uncle, look!"

"Those are sulfurous flames. They're perfectly normal in an eruption."

"But what if they come down on us?"

"They won't!"

"And what if that gas suffocates us?"

"It won't. You can see for yourself that the chimney's opening out."

"But the water . . . the boiling water!"

"There is no more water, Axel. We're on top of a sort of lava paste which is pushing us up to the mouth of the crater."

The heat was unbearable. I was drowning in sweat.

Suddenly we stopped moving. Had our raft got caught in something? I looked around, but our hellish ride had started again, faster than ever and jerkily too. I had to cling tight to the raft to avoid being thrown against the walls. I have no clear memory of the next few hours. All I have is a confused impression of continuous explosions and of being whirled around as if we were in a tornado. Our raft was sitting on a lava sea with hot ashes raining down around us. I thought I saw Hans' face one last time in the light of the

We went on rising at a frightening speed...

It's getting hotter and hotter. Almost forty degrees now!

Up to now, everything we have seen has confirmed Davy's theories. But nature's laws don't seem to apply to this world. The increase in temperature indicates that the rocks will start to melt soon. Hmm, it should be a fascinating experience!

I paid no attention to my uncle's ramblings. All I could think of was whether I would ever see my beloved Graüben again...

The water was now starting to boil and the walls of the shaft were beginning to alter in the intense heat. What would happen next?

What my uncle had to say made me shudder...

We're in the chimney of an erupting volcano, Axel, and right on top of the lava! We shall be ejected along with chunks of rock, ash and white-hot lava!

Is this volcano Sneffels? Have we returned to Iceland? Do you think we'll come out through Hecla or through one of the many other volcanoes on the island?

The shaft was getting narrower. The water had evaporated and we were now floating on boiling lava which was pushing us up towards the crater mouth...

The raft was being tossed about and was pitching violently on the lava sea. Our last hour had come! I lost consciousness...

When I opened my eyes again, we were out of the volcano!

Daylight! Thank God for that!

We're definitely not in Iceland, Hans! Where do you think we are?

We quenched our thirst at a little stream and were eating some fruit when a child came along and told us that we were on the island of Stromboli, in Italy.

menacing flames. A fiery hurricane enveloped us and I lost consciousness . . . .

When I opened my eyes again, I felt myself being supported by the guide's strong hand; he was holding on to my uncle with the other. I was not injured, apart from being bruised and weak. I was lying on a mountain slope, only a few paces from an abyss into which the slightest movement would have toppled me. It was Hans who had stopped us rolling farther down the side of the crater; he had saved our lives.

"Where are we?" asked my uncle, now he was fully conscious.

Hans shrugged his shoulders to show he did not know.

"In Iceland," I said.

"Nej," replied our guide.

"What do you mean, no?" exclaimed the Professor.

"Hans must be wrong," I agreed.

One last surprise awaited us. I had been expecting to see a northern landscape covered with perpetual snow and ice, weakly illuminated by the pale rays of the midnight sun, but instead I found a dry, sun-blistered mountain bathed in a fierce light. The three of us were sitting below the crater, looking out with stupefaction on a totally alien landscape. Once my eyes had become accustomed to the light, I tried to take my bearings.

"We must be in Spitsbergen, Uncle . . ."

"No, my boy. This volcano isn't in the north of the northern hemisphere — it hasn't a skullcap of snow!"

"Could it be Jan Mayen's Land?"

"Look, Axel, look!"

Above our heads was a volcanic crater through which, at regular intervals, a tall column of flame, mixed with ash and molten lava, emerged. The mountain was breathing like a whale which periodically spouts water from its huge blowers. Its base was encircled by a crown of green trees. Beyond them stretched the deep blue sea, sparkling in the sunlight.

"But where can we be then?" I asked several times.

We decided to move and after an easy two-hour descent we reached a magnificent stretch of country-side. Olive trees and fig trees stood alongside vines and pomegranates, and the fields looked as though they were lovingly tended. We quenched our thirst at a spring. While we were resting, a child suddenly appeared between two tree-trunks:

"Ah! Here's someone who can tell us!" I cried.

Frightened by the sight of these three dirty, ragged strangers, the boy took to his heels, but Hans ran after him and soon caught up with him.

● The walls were moving, rocks were falling and steam came out of the cracks.
●● He believed that, carried by the eruption, they would reach the surface of the earth again.
●●● Olive trees and fig trees.

My uncle tried to reassure the child, who must have thought we were devils, and asked him in German:

"What's the name of this mountain?"

The boy did not reply.

The Professor tried again in English.

The lad stared at us blankly.

"Let's try French," said my uncle.

But still he could not make himself understood.

But, translated into Italian, the question produced an answer.

"Stromboli!"

"Stromboli?"

"Yes, sir!" replied the child and, wriggling out of Hans' grip, he ran off through the olive trees.

That name produced a chain reaction in my mind. So, we were in the north of Sicily, not far from Etna, in the Aeolian chain of islands which Homer immortalized. As for the mountains we could see in the distance, they must be in Calabria! What an adventure! . . . We had gone in by a volcano in Iceland, and had come out from the bowels of the earth by another in Italy, far from the land of perpetual snow and Arctic frosts. My uncle turned to me with a broad grin and said:

"Poor Axel! And you were so sure you were going to die!"

Soon afterwards we marched off towards the little port of San Vicenzo.

What an amazing adventure! We went down through a volcano in Iceland and came up through Stromboli, more than three thousand miles from Sneffels! It's incredible!

You see? You were so sure you were going to die! Now, let's go down to the sea.

Some fishermen welcomed us and provided us with fresh clothes and food. We boarded a ship bound for Marseilles, then a train took us from there to Hamburg.

Martha's and Graüben's astonishment when they opened the door and saw us standing there defies description. Graüben cried her heart out, but they were tears of happiness.

Thanks to Martha's gossiping, the whole town soon learned of our return. No one would believe our story until we showed them our evidence. At last, a banquet was held in our honor...

Axel! You're famous now! Everyone thinks you're a great hero!

Hans became the center of attraction for those who wanted to learn more about our travels. He remained as we had always known him: cool, calm and level-headed.

My uncle presented Saknussemm's signed manuscript to the municipal archives, saying how sorry he was that he had been unable to follow in the illustrious scientist's footsteps right to the end. Despite this partial success, he emerged with an enhanced reputation.

One morning, without warning, Hans said goodbye. We were very fond of him and were sad to see him go. I hope that one day I shall see him again and shake him warmly by the hand.

A few days later, to my great joy, Graüben became my wife.

My wife now became mistress of the house at 19, Königsstrasse. Those of us who lived there remained happy and contented.

From that day on, my uncle was the most good-natured of scientists. The extraordinary adventure we had shared brought him a wealth of honorary titles and congratulations from mineralogical, geological and geographical societies throughout the world.

THE END

CHAPTER 13

30. Back home!

The fishermen who lived in the small community gave us a warm welcome and found us a change of clothing. One of them offered to take us to Messina, where a few days' rest did us the world of good. From there we caught a boat to Marseilles and then a train to Hamburg. On the evening of September 9 we arrived without warning at the door of No. 19 Königsstrasse. Martha answered our knock and almost fainted when she saw us. Graüben, who was right behind our cook, caught her as she was about to swoon. It is easy to imagine the excitement which our return caused. As a result of Martha's gossiping, the whole town soon knew all about the expedition, which had created quite a stir when we originally set out. But public interest had waned because of the lack of news of our progress. It was quite some time before our sceptical fellow–citizens could bring themselves to believe that we had actually made that fantastic journey from Iceland to Sicily underground. Then the congratulations came thick and fast. The town organized a great celebration in honor of the illustrious Professor Lidenbrock. He gave a lecture at the university and furnished a detailed account of our many adventures. That same day he deposited Saknussemm's manuscript in the city archives.

That evening Graüben said, when we were back inside the Königsstrasse house:

"Do you remember, Axel? When you left I told you that you would come back a man . . . And here you are, almost as famous as your uncle!"

The day came when Hans told us that he was going home. He shook us warmly by the hand and walked away, with that firm stride that I had come to know so well, never to return.

● He became the most placid and least irritable of scholars.

A few days later I became the happiest of men. Graüben, now my wife, took her place in No. 19 Königsstrasse as the lady of the house. As for my uncle, who had formerly been feared because of his difficult temperament and his tendency to fly into a rage, he is today the most placid and least irritable of scholars. Our joint adventure brought him a multitude of honorary titles bestowed on him by scientific, geographical and mineralogical societies throughout the world. He has succeeded in preserving his youthful and wonderful enthusiasm intact.

JULES VERNE, 1828-1905

He was born in Nantes, studied law in Paris, but decided to become a writer. He was one of the first novelists to write science fiction stories. His books, still popular in the space age, were actually written before the invention of the airplane.

He not only forecast the invention of submarines, airplanes, guided missiles, manmade satellites and television, but also accurately predicted their usage.

In the 1800's, there was a widespread interest in science which Verne took advantage of with his fantastic plots. His extensive knowledge of geography made his stories very realistic. With **Around the World in Eighty Days (1873), Journey to the Center of the Earth (1864), 20 000 Leagues Under the Sea (1870), From the Earth to the Moon (1865),** Verne carried his readers over the earth, under it and above it.

He used believable explanations and realistic details in his many incredible tales of adventure.